The First
Five Pages

Also by Noah Lukeman

The First Five Pages

A Writer's Guide to Staying
Out of the Rejection Pile

Noah Lukeman

OXFORD
UNIVERSITY PRESS

OXFORD
UNIVERSITY PRESS

Great Clarendon Street, Oxford, OX2 6DP,
United Kingdom

Oxford University Press is a department of the University of Oxford.
It furthers the University's objective of excellence in research, scholarship,
and education by publishing worldwide. Oxford is a registered trade mark of
Oxford University Press in the UK and in certain other countries

First published in hardback in the UK in 2000 by Robert Hale Ltd
This revised paperback edition published 2010

Published in the United States of America by Oxford University Press
198 Madison Avenue, New York, NY 10016, United States of America

British Library Cataloguing in Publication Data
Data available

Library of Congress Cataloging in Publication Data
Data available

ISBN 978-0-19-957528-2

Acknowledgements

A T Oxford University Press, I am indebted to Ben Harris, who had the vision and courage to give this book a second life in the UK. At Oxford, I would also like to thank Robert Faber, Vicki Donald, Rebecca Lane, Jamie Crowther, Helen Liebeck, Louise Corless, Juliet Evans, Chantal Peacock, Keira Dickinson, and Nick Clarke.

I would like to thank John Hale and Stella Wilkins for their support many years ago in the UK, and Caspian Dennis and Becky Thomas at Abner Stein for their efforts on behalf of this book now.

I would like to thank Daniel Myerson for his historical consultation, and Gene and Betsy Hackman for their early suggestions.

As always, I would like to thank my family for their endless support and love.

And most of all, I would like to thank the thousands of unpublished writers who taught me more about writing than I could ever imagine, and who are my daily inspiration.

The author gratefully acknowledges permission from the following sources to reprint material in their control: Pushcart Press for Andrée Bernard, ed., *Rotten Reviews*, 1986. *Icon* magazine for the excerpt from 'Conversations' with Martin Amis (June 1998). Allyn & Bacon for William Strunk and E. B. White, *The Elements of Style*, 3rd edn. Copyright © 1979. Johns Hopkins University Press for Louis Zukofsky, '*A*', pages 94–5. Copyright © 1993.

*For my mother, who, with unhesitating generosity,
showed my first (terrible) novel to her agent when
I was 16, and has supported my writing with
equal fervour ever since.*

Contents

In the interest of simplicity, I opt to use only the masculine. It is of course meant to refer equally to men and women.

Most honorable Sir,
We perused your MS.
with boundless delight. And
we hurry to swear by our ancestors
we have never read any other
that equals its mastery.
Were we to publish your work,
we could never presume again on
our public and name
to print books of a standard
not up to yours.
For we cannot imagine
that the next ten thousand years
will offer its ectype.
We must therefore refuse
your work that shines as it were in the sky
and beg you a thousand times
to pardon our fault
which impairs but our own offices.

                                                    Publishers

Rejection letter from a Chinese publisher, from Louis Zukofsky's '*A*'

Introduction

MOST people are against books on writing on principle. So am I. It's ridiculous to set down rules when it comes to art. Most of the truly great artists have broken all the rules, and this is precisely what has made them great. What would have become of Beethoven's music if he'd chased rules instead of inspiration? Of Van Gogh's paintings?

There are no rules to assure great writing, but there are ways to avoid bad writing. This, simply, is the focus of this book: to learn how to identify and avoid bad writing. We all fall prey to it, to different degrees, even the greatest writers, even in the midst of their greatest works. By scrutinizing the following examples of what *not* to do, you will learn to spot these ailments in your own writing; by working with the solutions and exercises, you may, over time, bridge the gap and come to a realization of what *to* do. There is no guarantee that you will come to this realization, but if you do, at least it will be your own. Because ultimately, the only person who can teach you about writing is yourself.

People are afraid to admit they'd dismiss a work of art instantaneously, whether it's the first five pages of an unsolicited manuscript or the first five pages of Faulkner. But the truth is they do. When it's a 'classic', most read on and finish the book to keep up pretext and not seem so presumptuous as to pass instant judgement on a great work. But they've secretly made up their mind after page 5, and 99 per cent of the time, they're not going to change it. It is not unlike the person who walks into a museum and dismisses Van Gogh in the flash of an eye; he would be scorned by critics, probably called a fool, but ultimately art is art, and this person has the right to pass his own judgement whether he's stared at it for a second or for a year.

In truth, though, this book is not concerned with the argument of whether one should dismiss a work of art instantaneously—this we'll leave to sophists—but rather, more simply, with whether a work is *technically* accomplished enough to merit a serious artistic evaluation to begin with. It is *not* like walking into a museum and judging the Van Goghs and Rembrandts; it is like walking into an elementary school art fair and judging which students exhibit more technical skill than others. An artistic evaluation is another, largely subjective can of worms. This book's objective is much simpler, much more humble. It is like a first reader who has been hired to make two piles of manuscripts, one that should be read beyond the first five pages and one that shouldn't. Ninety-nine per cent of today's unsolicited manuscripts will go into the latter. This book will tell you why.

When most professional literary agents and book editors hear the title of this book, they grab my arm, look me in the eyes and say, 'Thank you'. I can see their pent-up frustration at wanting to say so many things to writers and simply not having the time. I've come to understand this frustration over the last few years as I've read thousands of manuscripts, all, unbelievably, with exactly the same type of mistakes. From Texas to Oklahoma to California to England to Turkey to Japan, writers are doing *exactly the same things wrong*. While evaluating more than ten thousand manuscripts in the last few years, I was able to group these mistakes into categories; eventually, I was able to set forth definite criteria, an agenda for rejecting manuscripts. This is the core of *The First Five Pages*: my criteria revealed to you.

Thus, despite its title, this book is *not* just about the first five pages of your manuscript; rather, it assumes that by scrutinizing a few pages closely enough—particularly the *first* few—you can make a determination for the whole. It assumes that if you find one line of extraneous dialogue on page 1, you will likely find one line of extraneous dialogue on each page to come. This is not a wild assumption. Think of another art form—music, for example. If you listen to the first five minutes of a piece of music, you should be able to evaluate a musician's technical skill. A master musician would scoff at even that, saying he could evaluate a fellow musician's skill in five *seconds*, not five minutes. The master musician, through diligence and patience, has developed an acute enough ear to make an instant evaluation. This book will teach you the step-by-step criteria so that you, too, may develop that acute ear and make instant evaluations, be it of your own writing or of someone else's. By its end, you'll come to see why this book should not have been titled *The First Five Pages* but *The First Five Sentences*.

Agents and editors don't read manuscripts to enjoy them; they read solely with the goal of getting through the pile, solely with an eye to *dismiss* a manuscript—and believe me, they'll look for any reason they can, down to the last letter. I have thus arranged the following chapters in the order of what I look for when trying to dismiss a manuscript. You'll find that, unlike many books on writing, this book's perspective is truly that of the agent or editor.

Subsequently, I hope this book might also be useful to publishing professionals, particularly those entering the industry. Unlike other fields, publishing requires no advanced degrees; many neophytes, especially today, come straight from university or from media-related fields. Even if prospective agents or editors inherently know how to judge a manuscript—even if they have that 'touch'—in most cases they still won't be able to enunciate their reasoning beyond a vague 'this manuscript doesn't hold my interest'. It is crucial they know their precise reasons for rejecting a manuscript if they ever mean to talk about it intelligently. This book will help them in this regard. Everyone will ultimately develop his own order of elimination, his own personal pet peeves, and thus this book does not pretend to be the last word on the issue; but in its nineteen chapters, it covers many of the major points of a manuscript's initial evaluation.

Young publishing professionals must also keep in mind that, in some rare cases, the first five pages might be awful and the rest of the manuscript brilliant (and vice versa). They should thus not always keep too rigidly to the criteria and should also employ what I call the three-check method, which is, if the first five pages look terrible, check the manuscript a second time, somewhere in the middle, and then again a third time, somewhere towards the end. (It is extremely unlikely you will open to the only three terrible points in the manuscript.) This method should especially be employed if you are evaluating manuscripts for the first time and should be used until you feel supremely confident in the evaluation process.

The main audience for this book, though, is *you*, the writer. Along with the criteria, this book offers an in-depth look at the technique and thought processes behind writing and has been designed to be of interest to the beginning and more experienced writer alike, both as a general read and as a reference and workbook. There is so much to know in writing that even if you do already know it all, there are bound to be some things that have fallen to the back of your mind, some things you can use being reminded of. There is a lot of advice in this book; some you might use, some you might disagree with. Such is the nature of writing, which is, like all arts, subjective; all I can say is that if you walk away from these pages with even one idea that helps you with even one word of your writing, then it's been worth it. In the often frustrating business of writing—workshops, conferences, books, articles, seminars—this is a helpful principle to keep in mind.

You may feel uncomfortable thinking of yourself as a 'writer'. This is commonly encountered in new writers. They will often duck the label, insist they're not writers but have only written such and such because they had the idea in their head. There is a widely perpetuated myth that to be a 'writer', you need to have had many years' experience. Despite popular conviction, a writer needn't wear black, be unshaven, sickly, and waft around cocktail parties spewing aphorisms. You don't need to be a dead white male with a three-piece suit, noble countenance, smoking pipe, and curling moustache. And it has nothing to do with age. (I've seen twenty-year-old writers who've already been hard at work on their craft for five years and are brilliant, and sixty-year-old writers who have only been writing for a year or two and are still amateur. And, of course, one year for one writer, if he works ten hours a day on his craft, can be the equivalent of ten years for someone else who devotes but a few minutes a week.) All you need is the willingness to be labelled 'writer', and with one word you *are* a writer. Just as with one stroke, you are a painter; with one note, a musician.

This is a more serious problem than it may seem, because to reach the highest levels of the craft, above all you'll need *confidence*. Unshakeable confidence to leap forcefully into the realm of creation. It is daunting to create something new in the face of all the great literature that's preceded you; it may seem megalomaniacal to try to take your place on the shelf beside Dante and Faulkner. But maybe they once felt the same. The more we read, ingest new information, the greater the responsibility we have not to allow ourselves to succumb to the predicament Shakespeare described some three hundred years ago: 'art tongue-tied by authority'.

Of course, confidence is just the first step. The craft of writing must then be learned. The *art* of writing cannot be taught, but the *craft* of writing can. No one can teach you how to tap inspiration, how to gain vision and sensibility, but you can be taught to write lucidly, to present what you say in the most articulate and forceful way. Vision itself is useless without the technical means to record it.

There is no such thing as a great writer; there are only great *re*-writers. As you've heard before, 90 per cent of writing is rewriting. If first drafts existed of some of the classics, you'd find many of them to be dreadful. This process of rewriting draws heavily on editing. And editing can be taught. Thus the craft of writing, inspiration aside, *can* to a great extent be taught. Even the greatest writers had to have been taught. Did they know how to write when they were toddlers?

As an editor, you approach a book differently from a general reader. You should not enjoy it; rather you should feel like you're hard at work—your head should throb. You should constantly be on guard for what is wrong, what can be changed. You may relax only when you finish the book—but not even then, because more often than not you'll awake in the middle of the night three days later, remembering a comma that should have been on such and such a page. The only time an editor can truly relax is when the book is bound. Even then, he will not.

When an editor reads, he is not just reading but breaking sentences into fragments, worrying if the first half should be replaced with the second, if the middle fragment should be switched with the first. The better editors worry if entire sentences should be switched within paragraphs; great editors keep entire paragraphs—even pages—in their head and worry if these might be switched. Truly great editors can keep an entire book in their head and easily ponder the switching of any word to any place. They'll remember an echo across three hundred pages. If they're professional, they'll be able to keep ten such manuscripts in their head at once. And if you're the writer, and you call them a year later and ask about a detail, even though they've read five thousand manuscripts since then, they'll remember yours without a pause.

Master editors are artists themselves. They need to be. Not only can they perform all the tasks of a great editor, but they'll also bring something of their own to a text, give the writer a certain kind of guidance, let the writer know if a certain scene—artistically—should be cut, if the book should really begin on page 50, if the ending is too abrupt, if a character is underdeveloped. They'll never impose their will or edit for the sake of editing, but like a great actor, let it grow within them and then suggest changes that arise from the text itself. Like the great Zen master who creates priceless calligraphy with one stroke, the master editor can transform an entire page with one single, well-placed word.

But even if you become the master editor, you will still need a support group of astute readers to expose your work to fresh perspectives. This is a point I will raise many times throughout this book, so it is best if you can round them up now. These readers may or may not be in line with your own sensibility—it is good to have both—but they should be supportive of you, honest, critical, but always encouraging. Even the most proficient writers cannot catch all of their own mistakes, and even if they could, they would still be lacking the impartial reaction. Outside readers can see things you cannot. If you change one word due to their read, it's worth it.

Finally, this book differs from most books on writing in that it is not geared exclusively for the fiction or non-fiction writer, for the journalist or poet. Although some topics, to be sure, will be more relevant to certain types of writers and the majority of examples are from fiction, the principles are deliberately laid out in as broad a spectrum as possible, in order to be applied to virtually any form of writing. This should allow for a more interesting read, as writers of certain genres experiment with techniques they might not have considered otherwise, like the screenwriter grappling with viewpoint, the journalist with dialogue, the poet with pacing. It is always through the unexpected, the unorthodox, that artists break through to higher levels of performance.

Part I
Preliminary Problems

MANY writers spend the majority of their time devising their plot. What they don't seem to understand is that if their execution—if their *prose*—isn't up to par, their plot will never even be considered.

Agents and editors often ignore synopses and plot outlines; instead, we skip right to the actual manuscript. If the writing is good, *then* we'll go back and consider the synopsis. If not, the manuscript is discarded. A great writer can produce an amazing piece of writing with virtually no plot at all. To underline its relegated importance for the purpose of this book, you'll find we've deliberately omitted the chapter on plot.

Instead, as a way of emphasizing the importance, first and foremost, of the individual word, the *craft* of writing, we begin by first considering the preliminary problems that can be found in prose.

1

Presentation

Don't try to contact an editor or agent between 12:30 and 3. They will be lunching with other editors or agents. Don't contact them before lunch, because they will be settling in for the day. Don't contact them between 3 and 4, because they will be recovering from lunch and returning calls from those who called during lunch. Don't call them after 5, as Hollywood is finally waking up about then, and they are also preparing to leave for the day. So—if you absolutely must call—then call at exactly 4:30.

THIS is ultimately a book about writing, not publishing; thus to begin with presentation is nearly offensive, given its insignificance in the context of art (originally I had planned on not including it at all). But as the main purpose of this book is to lay out the criteria for rejecting a manuscript, I would be remiss not to include it—and not to put it first. It is inevitably the presentation that is looked at before all else in a manuscript, that can signal unprofessionalism to an agent or editor. So consider this chapter an exception.

It is a shame that small—and easily preventable—surface errors can be determinants for an entire book, can prematurely prevent you from being taken seriously. On the other hand, these smaller signs may be indicative of a certain broader sensibility: they may signal carelessness, sloppiness, ignorance or defiance of the industry's standards; that the writer doesn't care enough to do the minimum amount of research to make a manuscript industry presentable. Often when a writer's presentation is careless, his writing is too.

I remember once, as an agent, receiving a final manuscript from a writer to whom I had offered representation. I had been eagerly awaiting it and was disappointed when it arrived in a substandard format, printed on a dot-matrix printer, hard to read, filled with errors, even pagination mistakes. I asked her to make changes in order to put it into a more presentable form but, to my astonishment, she refused. She said, being low on funds, she had sold her computer to a pawn shop and had not bothered to keep either a disk or hard copy of the manuscript for herself. The copy in my hands—the one I had been about to discard—was the only one left in existence! I asked her why, being the veteran writer she was, she had not gone to the effort to put her manuscript into a more presentable format; she said she was aware of the industry's so-called standards but had a disdain for them, a disdain apparently reinforced by the fact that she had somehow managed to sell her first three manuscripts, all of which had been in a similarly sloppy format. I grudgingly made a rare exception and submitted it as it stood. It didn't sell.

You'll always find writers—and artists in general—who have an inherent disdain for 'industry standards' advice. They will point to manuscripts that have sold despite their poor condition. We all know these types: they are the actors who get the role without the head shot, the musicians who get the record deal without the demo tape. Don't let them influence you. You'll have enough obstacles as a writer, enough areas in which you can express yourself—don't let something as petty as formatting prevent you from being taken seriously. Agents and editors don't view someone who shies from the standards as unique or unusual, they view him as a nuisance, insensitive to their wishes. Your creativity should be expressed through your writing, not your font.

Context

Before we even get to the writing, it is important to first look at the *context* in which your manuscript is being judged. Like it or not, a manuscript's being taken seriously depends a great deal on who it is coming from. Stephen King's next novel would be read immediately by an agent; he would hold all calls and read it on the spot. A novel from an unknown writer, on the other hand, may sit in a pile for six months before it is even *opened*. More importantly, the agent reads a brand-name novelist's work with an eye for liking it, actively looks for reasons why it's good, and perhaps even blinds himself to its faults; the unknown writer's manuscript, however, will be read by an angry, overworked editorial assistant, one hoping to be able to find the tiniest fault so he can get it out of the way and move on to the next five thousand manuscripts.

There's not much you can do about not being Stephen King, but there are a few things you can do that may get you into a better pile—or at least get you a better position *within* the slush:

1. Devote extensive time to research. The number-one reason the aspiring writer gets rejected is because he has approached an agent or editor inappropriate for his work. This sounds obvious, but it amazes me how writers spend years working on their manuscripts but only *minutes* choosing which agent or editor to approach! In fact, I've never heard of a writer spending as much time researching agents or editors as he did writing his book.

Understandably, it is difficult for a writer to know who may or may not be appropriate. The publishing business is notoriously tight-lipped, and even if you do find the perfect match, this may work against you: occasionally, precisely *because* an agent or editor has already sold (or bought) a book like yours, he won't want to do another one. Still, an educated guess is better than a blind one. The internet can yield volumes of information, the single best site probably being www.publishersmarketplace.com. I've also written a free e-book which will help you greatly in this regard, and which can be downloaded at www.writeagreatquery. com. Use every method at your disposal. You'd be amazed at what time and effort can produce.

2. Let an agent or editor know why you're contacting him *specifically*. Now that you've done the research, use it. Most writers only go so far as to tell an agent, 'I read in such and such a guide that you handle "fiction", and thus am contacting you.' This is the most basic level of research; it will not impress an agent. Take it a step further. Use your advance research and be *specific*. A better way of catching an agent's eye is to tell him right off that you noticed he agented a specific title and that your manuscript is similar. An agent will appreciate that you've gone to the trouble, that you care; he will feel the submission is personalized and not part of a mass mailing. In return, he may treat you with personal care. The optimal way to approach, of course, is by referral, although this is not possible for all writers.

I remember once having received a letter from a writer who mentioned a literary novel I had agented, boasting how similar his novel was. I was impressed he'd gone to the trouble, and I looked at his manuscript right away. But his novel turned out to be a commercial thriller—one that could not possibly have been more different from the novel he'd referenced.

He'd obviously found out I'd sold the book but had not bothered to find out if his book really was similar at all! Don't refer to books just for the sake of it—only if truly appropriate.

3. Approach agents and editors with *care*. When most agents receive mail, they look at the return address. If it's a name they don't recognize, it goes on the pile, where it can sit for weeks or months without being opened. Editors are even more stringent: many of them send an unsolicited manuscript right back with a slip saying they won't consider it without an agent.

There are two things you can do about this. The first is to send only a one-page query letter with a stamped addressed envelope (sae). Small envelopes get opened, whereas oversized or overstuffed envelopes tend to get ignored or treated poorly. This partially stems from the fact that those of us who work in the industry are so overburdened with reading that we are terrified at the thought of having to open something of any *length*.

The second (which may or may not work) is to send your letter by some guaranteed-signature delivery method instead of by ordinary post. If it comes by a guaranteed-signature delivery method someone's forced to sign for it, and thus it usually gets opened on the spot. This doesn't guarantee it will get read—and the agent or editor may even get annoyed—but at least he'll be *aware* of it. Again, this may or may not work, and is certainly not mandatory—but if you can easily afford it, it is just one more option at your disposal.

How much is your time worth? £5 an hour? £10? £20? £100? How many hundreds of hours did you invest in the writing of your book? So, in this light, how much did it cost you to write your manuscript? Probably in the tens of thousands of pounds! (Not to mention the cost of paper, cartridges, photocopying, stationery, hardware.) Or you can look at it from another perspective: writers have few expenses compared to other artists. Painters can spend thousands on canvases and paints; musicians spend thousands on equipment and thousands more on recording. What does the writer need? Only his computer and his imagination. There are many areas I would *not* recommend spending on, but this—presentation—is one area where I would seriously consider spending. Ultimately, though, the point here is not to advocate the spending of money but to advocate the greater expenditure of personalized care.

Formatting

You've sent in your query letter and received an invitation from an agent or editor to send in your first few chapters or five (or ten or fifty) pages. Now let's move on to the presentation itself. Your manuscript may still be read with a prejudiced eye, or dismissed altogether. Here are a few things that can hinder you from getting off the ground:

- Paper. Your manuscript should be printed on A4, standard 80gsm white (not high-gloss) paper. Text should appear on only one side of the page. You will be stigmatized as amateur if the paper is stained, torn, or in any way defaced; if it is three-hole punched and/or bound in any way (screenwriters-turned-novelists often fall prey to this error, as this is the norm for screenplays—but *not* for book publishing); if the paper is some odd size; if the paper is coloured (including off-white) or 'grained'; if it is too thin (such as onionskin) or too thick. Finally, most commonly, if it is worn. Agents and editors are very sensitive to this; they look for even the slightest sign that someone has already read a manuscript. Often a manuscript comes in that is presentable in every way and is even clean and new-looking, but we can still spot tiny, tiny folds in the corners (or somewhere else along the borders) which indicate it has been read before (and thus rejected). We are suddenly predisposed against it. Just like that. Your years of hard work tainted because of such a minor thing.

I remember once receiving a terribly worn manuscript, covered in stains and so brittle the pages actually made a noise when I turned them. I was shocked a writer could be so careless and was about to reject it when I spotted a small Post-it in the corner, apologizing for the condition of the manuscript and attributing it to the fact that he, the writer, was currently in prison and thus unable to make new copies. So there are exceptions, and we must not take ourselves too seriously in the publishing business, must stray from our principles from time to time. And, of course, 'predisposed' does not mean 'predetermined', and I *have* offered representation to the worn manuscript. But why take the chance of hurting your odds if you can help it?

- Font. Your text should be printed in black ink, in a 12-point type font. A few things that may hurt you: if your font is too large (it will look abnormal) or too small (worse, it will be hard to read—the last thing you want to give to someone who is overburdened with reading). Since the 12-point font size differs from machine to machine, if you're unsure of the size, always err on the side of making your font too large. Other things that may count against you: if you use different fonts (some writers do this for emphasis, but it only makes it harder to read); if your manuscript is filled with boldface, underlined, capitalized, or italicized words everywhere (this is enough to drive an agent crazy! One look at a manuscript like this and it won't even be read); if your manuscript has fully justified margins; if your type is too dim, too dark, or printed on a dying cartridge; if your manuscript is printed on a dot-matrix printer. Most writers these days use inkjet or laser printers. I would strongly recommend investing in a laser printer—the inkjet is quickly becoming as second-class as dot-matrix used to be, and laser printers these days can be purchased for only a few hundred pounds.

- Spacing. Your manuscript should be double spaced, with one-inch margins. New paragraphs should be indented, as should dialogue. I would recommend starting halfway down the page whenever you begin a new chapter (these half pages give the illusion of turning pages quickly). A few things that will signal the amateur: if the manuscript is either single, one-and-a-half, or *more* than double spaced; if there is a line break between paragraphs (a common malady); if your margins are less or more than one inch in any direction (although it bothers many publishing professionals, I personally don't mind if margins are a little bit bigger—again, it just makes it easier to read); if your paragraphs or dialogue are not indented, or are indented at less (or more) than the normal tab key.

    You have no idea what a difference it makes for an over-read agent or editor to receive a beautiful-looking manuscript, printed cleanly on a laser printer, in a nice, easy-to-read font with plenty of spacing. I can't tell you how many times I've put off reading a manuscript simply because visually it was too hard to read.

- Miscellaneous. Additionally, there are several flourishes that can signal an amateur: if you include artwork or illustrations throughout the pages (if you truly want specific artwork or illustrations in the final book, then, after your book is sold, show them to the editor—often publishers will not want them, preferring to use their own illustrators); if you put on the first or title page what 'rights' you're offering—most writers don't know anything about rights, they just stamp this on because it sounds fancy. In actuality, when you present a manuscript to an agent or editor, you are offering all rights (except in a very few cases). Then there is what I call the 'paranoid' manuscript, with 'Copyright' or '©' or 'Confidential' stamped on every page. Agents and editors are not going to steal your ideas—they have enough to worry about. As a writer myself, I'm never worried about an agent or editor stealing my idea, because just stealing it won't get them anywhere. They still have to convince a publisher. And that's not easy!

Textual Odds and Ends

Even if the formatting is perfect, there are other odds and ends that can cause a preliminary dismissal. Perhaps the single biggest one is the question mark. Ninety-nine per cent of the time it is misused, especially when it appears early and often. Usually finding one of these is enough to dismiss a manuscript (not to mention a manuscript filled with them). The same holds true for the exclamation mark. To a lesser degree, the same holds true for parentheses, although, since more easily fixed, this is really only a problem if severely overused.

There are also textual odds and ends that might not necessarily signal an amateur but which can put off a reader immediately. These include affectations, such as the abundant use of foreign words or phrases, or the inappropriate use of fancy words; crude or vulgar language or images; graphic blood and sex; and most commonly, the cliché. I can't tell you how many manuscripts either open with clichés or have one on their first page. This is almost always a sure indicator of a commonplace sensibility and will thus lead to instant rejection.

Now your presentation is perfect. You're being read. Your moment in the spotlight has come. It's time to look at the prose itself, to see if you can make it past the first five pages.

2

Adjectives and Adverbs

The serious fiction writer will think that any story that can be entirely explained by the adequate motivation of the characters or by a believable imitation of a way of life or by a proper theology, will not be a large enough story for him to occupy himself with. This is not to say that he doesn't have to be concerned with adequate motivation or accurate reference or a right theology; he does; but he has to be concerned with them only because the meaning of his story does not begin except at a depth where these things have been exhausted.

Flannery O'Connor, from an essay, 1957

modifier, n. *That which modifies.*

adjective, n. *A word used to modify a noun. For instance, in the phrase,* 'a wise *ruler',* wise *is the adjective.*

adverb, n. *A word used to modify a verb. For instance, in the phrase,* 'he ran quickly', quickly *is the adverb.*

AFTER its presentation, the quickest and easiest way to reject a manuscript is to look for the overuse, or misuse, of adjectives and adverbs. Most people who come to writing for the first time think they bring their nouns and verbs to life by piling on adjectives and adverbs, that by describing a day as being 'hot, dry, bright, and dusty' they make it more vivid. Almost always the opposite is true.

Here are six reasons why manuscripts heavy on adjectives and adverbs generally don't work:

1. More is less. When a string of adjectives or adverbs is used, they detract from each other. It is difficult, if not impossible, for a reader to keep all those modifiers in his head by the time he gets to the noun or verb.
2. It can be demeaning to the reader when the writer fills in every last detail for him. It assumes he has no imagination of his own. As readers, we bring so many of our own associations to the table anyway, we're going to substitute our own picture of a car, say, no matter how much effort a writer puts into describing it.
3. It is often preferable to leave things blank and force the reader to use his imagination—that way he makes the text his own, becomes more fully engaged in the manuscript. He won't set it down if it's *his*.
4. Writers who overuse adjectives and adverbs tend to use commonplace ones—usually ones they've heard used in the same context before—and the hackneyed result is immediately apparent. (It is rare to find truly unusual adjectives or adverbs in a manuscript.)
5. Adjectives and adverbs often, ironically, *weaken* their subjects. It is as if the writer were saying to the reader, 'This noun (or verb) is not strong enough to stand on its own, so I will modify it (or build it up) with a few adjectives (or adverbs).'
6. Finally, the overall effect of a text encumbered with adjectives, adverbs, and the inevitable commas in between makes for very slow, awkward reading—which these writers would find out for themselves if they only took the time to read their own work aloud.

Manuscripts heavy on adjectives or adverbs can be spotted by an agent or editor immediately—sometimes even in the first few sentences—by looking for a plethora of commas (which inevitably separate a string of adjectives), or in the case of a writer who doesn't even know how to use commas, by looking to the nouns and verbs and then looking to see if adjectives or adverbs precede (or succeed) them.

Solutions

The good news is that a manuscript adjective or adverb heavy is also easy to fix. A few simple solutions you can implement right now:

- Cut back your usage. Amazingly, you can improve your prose simply by going through your manuscript (with an eye for this) and reducing the sheer number of adjectives and adverbs. When deciding where to cut, there are three places you can look: (1) places where you use more than one adjective or adverb. Remove all but one. When deciding which one to keep, ask yourself which is the strongest, the most unusual; ask yourself, if you could link only one adjective or adverb with the noun or verb, which would be most important? You'll often find that there *is* one idea that is more pressing to convey than the others. For instance, taking your 'hot, dry, bright, and dusty day', you might decide it's most important to describe your day as 'bright'. Yes, you lose something by not having those other adjectives—but is it worse to lose something, or not to be read at all? (2) places where you've used commonplace or clichéd adjectives—a 'hot' day, for instance—and cut these; and (3) places where you've used any unusual nouns or verbs. (If these are strong enough, they need not be modified by an adjective or adverb.)
- Replace your existing adjectives and adverbs with more unusual ones. Now that you've cut the excess adjectives and

adverbs, turn your attention to the ones that remain. Chances are that in each instance you'll be able to come up with a more unusual, less expected replacement. On a small scale this may not seem to make a difference, but in the bigger picture it does: the cumulative feel of a three-hundred-page manuscript littered with commonplace adjectives and adverbs is, well, commonplace.

- Strengthen your nouns and verbs so that they don't need adjectives and adverbs. You could say 'He was a brutal man,' or 'He was a tyrant'; you could say 'She was a kind, charitable woman,' or 'She was a saint'; you could say 'It was a torrential rain,' or 'It was a downpour'; you could say 'He was running quickly,' or 'He was sprinting.' In the same way that you can find better adjectives or adverbs, at least some of the time you should be able to come up with stronger (or more precise) nouns or verbs that can make adjectives and adverbs unnecessary to begin with. *When rewriting, pretend someone will give you £100 for every word you are able to cut.* You will be able to cut scores of adjectives and adverbs just by strengthening their subjects, making for a much tighter manuscript.

- Occasionally substitute a comparison (analogy, simile, or metaphor) for an adjective. You can say 'He ran a clean, well-organized office,' or 'He ran his office like a ship'; you can say 'The man was tall, heavy, overgrown,' or 'The man was built like a bear'; you can say 'He ate ravenously, without any decorum,' or 'He ate like an animal.' You don't want to replace every adjective or adverb in your manuscript with a comparison, but occasionally it works well, further reducing the number of modifiers and simultaneously filling your manuscript with visuals. It also may reduce the sheer number of words, which makes for a tighter read.

Examples

*The squad car went **fast** down the **bumpy, rocky road, quickly** swerving to avoid the **large, fat** insects smashing **squarely** against the **slimy** windscreen. The **hot, humid, stifling** day poured in **in waves** through the **open** windows, making the men wipe their **sweaty, clammy** brows with their **dirty, greasy** rags and leaving marks along their **dirty** foreheads. The convict was escaping quickly and it was getting hard to see in the **blinding** haze.*

*Finally, they pulled him over to the **left** side of the road, their brakes **squealing and screeching**. They emerged **hastily**, running **quickly** over to the **long, dark, old** Cadillac. They **slowly** pulled out their flashlights and shone them **brightly** on to the **pale, confused, startled** face inside the car. One cop pulled out his **big, heavy, metal** gun and held it **high** above his head; the other reached for his **sleek, silver** handcuffs and dangled them **dangerously** in front of the **wary, apprehensive** face of the car's occupant. They yelled **loudly** for the **car's occupant** to get out of the car, and the door opened **slowly, cautiously, squeaking, rattling, and shaking**.*

There are numerous problems with this paragraph—not just adjectives and adverbs—but I've tried to focus on just these, underscoring problem areas that could be either cut or replaced with something better. In line 1, 'went fast' could be 'sped'; 'bumpy' and 'rocky', while slightly different, both convey the same idea, and so one of them can be cut; if a car is speeding down a highway and 'swerving', we know that it's doing it 'quickly', and so this adverb can be cut; again, 'large' and 'fat', line 2, convey the same idea, so one can be cut (incidentally, it would also be preferable to replace 'insects' with the specific *type* of insects that are hitting the windscreen— the more specific you can be in writing, the better); the chances are, if the insects are 'smashing' against the windscreen, they are smashing 'squarely', and so this adverb can be cut, and if the bugs are smashing against it, the windscreen must be 'slimy', and so this adjective can be cut. And so on ... The reasons for the remainder of the underscoring should be self-evident, except I'll point out that in line 3, 'in waves' is a cliché and is not really necessary, and if the air is pouring in, then we know the windows are 'open'. In line 12, 'pale, confused, startled'—it is obvious that either 'confused' or 'startled' will convey the same general idea, but what about 'pale'? This, you might say, is a totally different idea and thus there *must* be two adjectives here. Well, it is a different idea, but in cases like this, you'll just have to decide which is more important in that moment: to convey that the convict is 'pale' or that he is 'startled'. You're not always going. to be able to convey everything you want, but at least you'll have a much tighter manuscript, and in the long run it will pay off. Let's look at the same example, revised:

> *The squad car sped down the rocky road, swerving to avoid the locusts smashing against the windscreen. The stifling day poured in through the windows, making the men wipe their clammy brows with rags, leaving marks along their foreheads. The convict was escaping, and it was getting hard to see in the haze.*
>
> *Finally they pulled him over, their brakes squealing. They emerged hastily, running to the dark Cadillac. They pulled out their flashlights and shone them on to the confused face inside the car. One cop pulled out his gun and held it above his head; the other reached for his handcuffs and dangled them in front of the apprehensive face. They yelled for the car's occupant to get out. The door opened slowly, squeaking.*

This is still far from Tolstoy—and numerous problems still remain—but at least, without all the adjectives and adverbs, it is slightly more readable. Notice how all the major ideas are still conveyed without them.

> *In the **dark, cold, restraining** jail, John felt **sad, angry, and hurt** that no one had come to visit him. He paced **up and down** and grabbed **tightly** on to the **long, circular** bars. He tried to stick his head through the **small, narrow** spaces between the bars but it wouldn't fit **completely**. He yelled **loudly** for someone to answer him, but all he heard **back** were the **laughing, sardonic, mocking** voices of the other inmates **next door**. He sat on his **long, metal, uncomfortable** bed and put his head in his hands, sobbing **hysterically** and **shaking** and perspiring **greatly**.*

As is often the case, there are so many problems with this example, it's hard to focus on just the adjectives and adverbs. In line 1, 'dark, cold, restraining' is a good example of three separate ideas, only one of which should remain. 'Restraining' can go, because what else can a jail be? So it's between 'dark' and 'cold', both of which are commonplace. But if we had to choose, I would go with 'dark', because cold can be conveyed by many other aspects of the jail, such as the bars or the bed or the floor. (In general, when you're torn as to which adjective to give up, scan the text to see if you might convey one of the ideas elsewhere.) For 'sad, angry, and hurt', the writer's just going to have to decide which is the dominant feeling. It should be obvious why most of the other words are marked, but I'll mention that in line 2, 'up and down' is an example of a clichéd modifier associated with the verb, one which can often be cut (in the previous example, the air coming in 'in waves' was another), and in line 7, 'next door' is an example of an unnecessary modifier, because where else could the other inmates be?

> *In the **bright, shiny** sky there appeared two **large, massive** birds, circling **slowly** around the **young, scared** rabbit. It ran **quickly**, jumping **bravely** over **small, sharp** rocks and trying to make its way **desperately** to its **little** hole. The birds dived **ferociously** and*

*with **long, sharp** claws grabbed the baby rabbit's **short, white** hair and swept him up **pridefully** into the **large, open** sky. They flew **victoriously** back home, their **wide, black, slick** wings reflecting the **hot afternoon** sun.*

By now, many of these adjective/adverb errors should be evident. The ones that are slightly more subtle are: in line 2, 'slowly' is an example of an adverb that can be cut altogether—if they're circling, we know it's slowly. This is important, because not all bad adjectives or adverbs should be replaced—some should be cut altogether, always the preferable route. 'Bravely', in line 3, is a good example of a writer not giving the reader the benefit of the doubt, not crediting him with the imagination to visualize the rabbit's attempted escape. And in the final line, 'hot' is a good example of an adjective that is not serving the purpose of the sentence. If you backtrack, you'll see that the gist here is that the wings are 'reflecting' the sun. Thus, an adjective, if any, used to modify the sun should be associated with 'reflecting', e.g. 'bright', but not 'hot'.

End-of-Chapter Exercises

Now you're aware of the extent of the adjective and adverb problem and have some practical ways of approaching it, I'd like to give you some exercises (as I will at the end of every chapter), not to address any one problem in particular (as we did in the examples), but to help you grapple further with the issue as a whole.

These exercises may be done alone or with a partner or group; at your leisure or immediately. The only rule is this: Do not go on to the next chapter until you've actually done these exercises at least once.

- Remove every adjective and adverb from the first page of your manuscript and list them separately. How many are there? Now read the first page aloud (without the adjectives or adverbs). How does it read? Faster? Are your major ideas still conveyed without them?

- Look at your list of removed adjectives and adverbs. How many are commonplace or clichéd? Cross out each one and beside it write down a less expected replacement. Now go back to your first page and insert your replacements. Read it aloud. How does it read now?

- Remove every noun and verb from the first page of your manuscript and list them separately. How many are commonplace or clichéd? Cross out each one and beside it write down a less expected replacement. Now go back to your first page and insert your replacements. Read it aloud. How does it read now?

- Finally, rewrite the first page completely, abiding by the rule that you cannot use any adjectives or adverbs. Watch how this forces you to come up with nouns and verbs that have to stand on their own, without any support from adjectives and adverbs. What are the differences? Can any of these be incorporated?

3

Sound

Vigorous writing is concise. A sentence should contain no
unnecessary words, a paragraph no unnecessary sentences, for
the same reason that a drawing should have no unnecessary
lines and a machine no unnecessary parts. This requires not that
the writer make all his sentences short, or that he avoid all detail
and treat his subjects only in outline, but that every word tell.

William Strunk and E. B. White, *The Elements of Style*

THIS chapter forms a demarcation: the first two chapters
covered ailments an agent or editor could detect based
upon a surface *glance* at a manuscript. But to evaluate
sound, even on the crudest level, the agent or editor must actually
give a manuscript a surface *read*, enter the text, let the words, for
good or for bad, ring in his head. So, if you've made it this far,
you're getting there.

There *is* a sound to prose; writing is not just about getting a
story across, but also—if not mainly—about *how* you get there.
Prose can be technically correct but rhythmically unpleasant. This
is one of the distinctions between writing in general and writing
as an art form. We've all encountered the ill-sounding sentence,
most commonly found in the run-on. Technically it's correct, but
it just 'sounds' wrong. Indeed, what I label sound may also be
thought of as 'rhythm'.

Accomplished poets often make the best writers of prose because they bring to their art years of paying close attention to the sound of language, to its rhythm, breaks, to subtle elements like alliterations and echoes. They can spend years working on just one *line*, and this devotion to the craft of the individual word almost always translates into immaculate prose, beautiful to hear and beautiful to read.

If you strike the right notes on a piano and let them reverberate, you will, if you listen very closely, hear the 'waves' beneath the music. Musical notes do not, as most people think, ring steadily; they reverberate in tiny waves, always growing louder and softer. The same holds true of prose: beneath the text there lurks a wave of sound, one that must always be monitored, tempered.

There are myriad levels of sound problems—from overt to subtle—and so this chapter is relevant to both beginner and expert. Sound comes among the first considerations because the ill-sounding manuscript is instantly recognizable. Sound problems begin with sentences that are poorly constructed and divided, the most elementary form of grammatical misusage—so elementary, in fact, it is actually rare to find a manuscript with overtly terrible sound.

But sound problems can also trouble the expert. He will clearly know how to form a sentence—may even form a nice-sounding sentence—but he may be less conscious of things like subtle echoes or distasteful consonants or vowels. Every writer, like every artist, has his strong and weak points: many writers who are otherwise quite good often don't pay as much attention to sound as they should, focused as they are on things like plot, characterization, setting. Of course, there are only so many things a writer can keep in his head at once. Many writers first want to get their story down and then worry about things like sound upon revision. But after one or two revisions, the writer will inevitably begin to hate his own work; the sentences will begin to sound the same and he'll quickly lose perspective. So it is not uncommon for even the greatest writer to have at least minor sound afflictions—be it one word every thirty pages—that can be handled with good editing from an outside reader.

Sound can be one of the harder problems to diagnose. Here are a few of its more common manifestations:

• Poor sentence construction. On the most basic level, sound problems arise out of simple grammatical mistakes in sentence construction. Poorly constructed sentences will seem to a lay reader to 'make no sense'; he may read a sentence repeatedly and still not get it. Watch him as he reads: he will first wrinkle his brow, then frown in frustration, then drop the manuscript in anger. The symptoms are sentences that seem too long, too short. But the underlying cause, most often, is that the sentences are not well divided. To be even more specific, the root of this poor division is the misuse of commas, full stops, colons, semicolons, dashes, and parentheses.

It is my experience that nearly everyone knows how to use the full stop and most people know how to use the comma, most of the time. But you would be amazed at how many people use the comma poorly at least some of the time (the difference between proficiency and mastery) and more amazed at how few people really know how to use the semicolon, colon, dash, and parentheses for optimal effect. For your convenience, here is a brief rundown:

The **semicolon** should be used to connect two (or more) sentences or ideas that are distinct but closely related. These two (or more) sentences should not be so similar that they warrant being merged (with, say, a comma and a conjunction) and yet they should also not be distinct enough to be separated (by a full stop). Thus, you use the semicolon. (The semicolon has other uses too, such as when listing or numbering ideas.) It is worth looking at *Moby-Dick* to see how Melville employs the semicolon. One critic of the 1800s criticized Melville's usage; perhaps he was right. But still, after reading eight hundred pages of *Moby-Dick*'s sentences, it's hard to imagine a sentence without one.

The **colon** should be used when you want to offset a point clearly. It can also be used to replace the phrase 'that is'. For instance: 'All of his actions pointed to one thing: he was a mean man.' In this example, the colon replaces the phrase 'that is' (offset by commas). The colon should also be used before listing items, as in 'I bought three things at the shop: soap, toothpaste, and a bar of chocolate.' (The colon also has other uses, such as to separate a title from its subtitle, to initiate a formal letter, etc.)

The **dash** basically serves the same purpose as the colon, without the formality. I say basically, because it differs in two ways: (1) you might use the dash to denote an afterthought to a sentence. For instance: 'This product is great—it's amazing, actually.' In this case, you would not use the colon. And (2) unlike the colon, dashes are frequently used in pairs, to offset a clarification (or tangent) in the midst of a sentence. For instance: 'I was running in the rain—I had forgotten my umbrella—when I saw the vendor.' In this case, 'I had forgotten my umbrella' clarifies why the subject was running.

A common mistake is to confuse the **hyphen** with the dash. The hyphen is one mark '-', the dash is typed as two '--'; the hyphen is used to connect some compound words or indicate that a word is broken by the margin and will continue on the next line.

Parentheses serve almost the same purpose as pairs of dashes: they are used as a way of including a clarification or tangent in the midst of a sentence. They differ slightly in that they are more formal than dashes, and are often used to imply an afterthought. They should also be used less frequently, as they are stylistic. If overdone, they can often be effectively replaced by dashes.

- Echoes. The echo problem is most commonly found in three forms: (1) character names (when a character's name is repeated too often); (2) the words 'he' and 'she' (when either 'he' or 'she' is substituted for a character name but then ends up being used too much itself); and (3) unusual words (often writers end up seizing on some unusual word and using it at least a few times throughout a text).

- Alliteration. Technically, alliteration is the repetition of the first letter or sound of a word in the first letter or sound of a word following it (either immediately or a few words later)— for instance, 'the *l*arge *l*ock' or '*w*alking down the *w*ide street'. I once studied under a professor of Shakespeare who argued that alliteration can be even more subtle, should also include sound picked up from the middle and even ends of words, for instance, '*e*loquent *q*uixotic'. No matter how used, alliterations have a strong presence and must be tempered. When overused they can make a manuscript sound juvenile, like forced poetry. (Of course, we need not even mention rhymes in prose manuscripts, which should be avoided at all cost.)

- Resonance. To climb the subtlety ladder, a more advanced usage (or misusage) of sound comes in the form of resonance, that is, the way a sentence resounds within the context of a paragraph (or line break or chapter). For instance, if you have a series of long sentences and then one short one, this short sentence will resonate differently from the way it would have if the other sentences had also been short. But resonance can also apply to the beginning and middle of paragraphs and even to individual words. This gets tricky, because everything in writing is relative, and a short sentence beside another short one may not necessarily work, whereas it might beside a long one.

Solutions

In general, a sound problem is difficult to fix by yourself because, since you were the one who wrote the words, they will most likely 'sound' fine when you read them back. Also, you already know your sentences by heart (or at least well) and so will not scrutinize them upon a further read but, rather, mentally fill in the gaps. However, here are some solutions:

- The most effective solution will be to give your manuscript to a trusted reader, specifically asking him to read just for sound. Ask him in advance to tell you if there are any places it 'sounds' wrong; any sentences that are confusing, that seem too long, too short, or poorly divided; any echoes, any repetitions that bother him; any difficulties grasping the meaning of any sentences.
- Read your manuscript aloud. Playwrights always say they can never tell anything about their play until they've heard it read out loud; to a lesser degree, the same holds true for prose. When it comes to sound, you can turn yourself into an outside, discriminating reader simply by switching the voice in your head with the one in your throat. Did you stumble anywhere? What felt wrong? Reading aloud, if done genuinely, will almost always bring out any awkward sentence fragments. Experiment with altering, moving, or cutting them.
- Cut. Most sound problems, including repetition, echoes, alliteration, rhymes, and poor sentence fragments, can be fixed by simple cutting. Actually how to write harmonious prose is beyond the scope of this book, but at least the offensive passages will be removed.

- Simplify. Most writers equate complexity of thought with complexity of sentence structure. A huge mistake. On the contrary, it is much harder to present complex ideas in a straightforward manner. Personally, I am always more impressed by simplicity, clarity; it is the mark of a writer who knows his subject well and is secure enough not to 'lay it on' in the telling. Aim for complexity of thought, not expression. Even if your sentence sounds great, always ask yourself if its meaning is clear for the reader.

Examples

While walking in the park he came across them sitting down on the bench under the tree beside the litter bin. He wanted to approach them but he saw they were watching him so he turned to the side still watching them while he turned and walked away to the other end of the park. He saw the only way to approach them without them seeing him would be for him to approach them from behind that way they would not notice if he approached them. He walked around in one big circle before coming back then he sneaked up on them from behind he walked quietly so they wouldn't hear while he did they were surprised completely when he sat down. They leapt up from the bench and ran from him he leapt up from the bench and followed them they went down the boardwalk like this for some hours. Until finally a policeman came alerted by the people. The people complained to the police and they threatened to put the man in jail but he cried and they said ok get out of here.

As I said before, one of the main ways you know you're looking at a sentence that is poorly constructed is that it is hard to understand—even after a few readings, you might not be sure what's meant. The simple act of dividing a sentence can give you tremendous editorial power—it's amazing. The same sentence, divided in five different ways, can mean five different things. One of the reasons a poorly constructed sentence is so hard to understand is that you can read it in different ways—none of them necessarily wrong. It is like a half-drawn picture.

In line 1, 'them' should be followed by a full stop. At first glance, it may seem like a comma would do, but if you read the remainder of the sentence, you'll see a full stop is necessary because of the long string of modifiers that applies to 'them'. (Of course, if a full stop is used, a bridge, such as 'They were', will be needed for a smooth transition into the next sentence.) Commas are the most subjective of all dividers, but I would say that two of them are necessary in the blanks in line 2, between 'bench' and 'under', and 'tree' and 'beside', because of the long string of modifiers. A comma is necessary in the first blank in line 4 between 'side' and 'still', and a comma again in the second blank in line 4, between 'turned' and 'and'. Full stops are needed in the blanks between lines 8 and 9, between 'back' and 'then', in line 9, between 'behind' and 'he', and in line 10, between 'did' and 'they'. In line 13, 'Until' is a good example of where a sentence should actually be made longer, deleting the full stop and replacing it with a comma. The rest should be self-evident, except I'll mention in lines 14, 15, and 16, all these blanks are a good example of places where the use of commas would be subjective, depending on the mood and style of the piece.

__Little__ __L__arry leapt all up and down the __yard__ __y__elping like the little child that he was. __He held his head up h__igh but __everyone who was anyone__ could tell he liked to yell for the __sorry s__ake of it. Why was he __running r__ampant like a little boy? This was because he __wanted what no one wanted__ to __go and g__ive him, which was a __paltry p__iece of attention. Wishing he could walk like *a **burgeoning b**oy, **Larry l**eapt all the way to the **sacred s**chool, carrying his books and cursing like a **rabid r**odent. Little Larry was **happily h**eralded by his **big b**rute friends who knew he liked to chew his **plentiful p**encils in class, which he carried with him in his **big b**ag like **some s**ort of **wielded w**eapon. Little Larry **poked the p**recious teacher with his **p**encil until she **cursed and cried and c**alled the **precious p**rincipal who **suddenly s**tormed into the **cackling c**lassroom and demanded all the **bad b**oys leave immediately, especially Larry.*

This is a perhaps hyperbolic example of alliteration at work (or, I should say, *not* at work). But by exaggerating it, we can really *hear* the sound of the prose, can see that prose *does* have a sound. Your writing may use (or misuse) sound to a lesser degree, but it is there, and the more you look for it, the easier it will be to find. If you stay on this track, you will eventually find yourself reading as much for sound as you do for content. It's like listening to a song: do you listen for the melody or the words? It's always a combination, but often the melody, the *sound*, is dominant. This can become a danger, too, as beautiful prose can veil paucity of content.

The problems in the above example should be apparent, but I'll mention a few that may not be: in lines 2–3, 'everyone who was anyone' is neither an alliteration nor a true rhyme, but a semi-rhyme and a good example of an echo; in lines 12–13, 'cursed and cried and called'—take note that alliterations don't necessarily need to be one after the other—sometimes they can be spread out over entire sentences; and note the echo of the unusual usage of the word 'precious', also in line 13. Throughout you'll notice many adjectives that are not quite right, such as 'sorry sake' in line 3 and 'burgeoning boy' in line 7. This is what rhyming and alliteration can do to a lesser writer: his main priority becomes the sound of the language, and for this he sacrifices content, meaning, and precision of thought.

> *John Spinoza ate what was left of the cake that Mary Charle-son had brought. John liked the cake but John thought it tasted strange and thought Mary strange for bringing it. Mary had brought it with good intentions but Mary didn't exactly know what John's tastes were. John actually scowled when he opened it because John's temperament is so much against the sort of cake that Mary brought.*
>
> *When she left, he watched her from the window and then he got up and he walked around his flat. He sat down and he got up and he walked around some more while he watched the insects crawl on the wall. She had done it this time by her not bringing his favourite cake. She knew she would get him mad, she did, but she brought it anyway and she should have thought and she shouldn't have brought it.*

A classic example of the overuse of character names and 'he/she'. Technically, the writer's done nothing wrong, but rhythmically, it is unpleasant. This is also a good example of what I have been referring to as the echo. Remember: reading is a cumulative experience. As he proceeds, a reader unconsciously stores in his head all the words in your manuscript. Echoes, to the discerning reader, will take their toll.

The good news is that character name and he/she echoes are among the easiest problems to fix. Most of the time, a character name can simply be replaced by 'he/she'. The 'he/she' can usually be fixed by simple deletion—the trick is finding the best way to bridge the gap left by the deletion. The use of a character's *full* name should probably only come once or twice in an entire book, if at all, and usually only when first introducing him. For instance, if we already knew these characters but the writer, regardless, used their full names, as he did in line 1, then this would be a mistake.

End-of-Chapter Exercises

An ear for sound is developed over time. Don't get frustrated; it will happen. It will most likely not happen overnight, but one day you'll be reading (your work or someone else's) and you'll realize you're reading as much—if not more—for sound as you are for content.

- To begin, let's focus on something you've already written. Take one paragraph from the first five pages (it may be the first paragraph, but only if you haven't already bludgeoned it to death) and devote at least four working hours to it. Revise it with an eye towards making it 'sound' as pleasing as possible. Often such focused time and attention alone offers a whole new perspective—it makes the individual word, sentence, and paragraph so much more important. When you approach the rest of your work after this exercise, you'll do it with reverence, with incomparably more care and thoughtfulness.
- Take some time to read poetry. Spend weeks reading as many different poets as you can. By devoting all this attention to the individual word, phrase, and stanza, you will learn a greater attention for language, and this attention will eventually show in your own work.
- Having read your poets, take a paragraph or section from your first five pages and reformat it on the page as if it were a poem. Where would you put the stanza breaks? What words would you change if it were a poem? Would you delete anything, add anything, make anything tighter, expand on any ideas? Now, putting the paragraph back to normal, can you implement any of the changes?

4

Comparison

Muddiness is not merely a disturber of prose, it is also a destroyer of life, of hope: death on the highway caused by a badly worded road sign, heartbreak among lovers caused by a misplaced phrase in a well-intentioned letter, anguish of a traveler expecting to be met at a railroad station and not being met because of a slipshod telegram.

> William Strunk and E. B. White, *The Elements of Style*

analogy, n. *A likeness between things when the things are otherwise entirely different. For instance, 'learning is to the mind what light is to the eye, enabling it to discover things hidden'. In this case, an analogy is drawn between 'learning' and 'light'.*

simile, n. *The likening of two things, generally by using the words 'like' or 'as', which, however different, have some strong point of resemblance. A poetic or imaginative comparison.*

metaphor, n. *A comparison is implied but not formally expressed. A short simile. Thus, 'that man is like a fox' is a simile; but 'that man is a fox' is a metaphor.*

A PICTURE is worth a thousand words, and when you use a comparison (by 'comparison' I mean analogy, simile, or metaphor) you draw a picture, often with the goal of helping the reader grasp a difficult idea. Comparison is one of the few devices that really put a writer's skill in the spotlight because it offers the most room for a writer to 'turn it on', to indulge the limits of his creative expression. It is not without reason that the dictionary defines a 'simile' as a 'poetic or imaginative comparison'. And the metaphor is an even higher art form than the simile. More concise, more bold, the metaphor uses fewer words to express the same thing, the aim of all good writing.

The proper use of comparison will enable you to cut a tremendous amount of description (which inevitably slows your book down). It will save you literally pages of work and make for a much tighter read. For all you self-indulgent stylists out there, consider channelling your flair into the comparison. Not so easy.

While the benefits of comparison for the skilled writer can be huge, the consequences of badly worded comparison for a lesser writer can be disastrous. You must remember that when you use comparison you tell a reader to stop, you draw attention to a particular idea, and if it is not apt, you'll draw magnified attention to your imprecision. Bad or clichéd comparisons jump off the page. They indicate imprecision or laziness in searching for the right picture—both of which have no place in a writer's work. This is why a manuscript misusing comparison can be dismissed so quickly, why this chapter comes fourth out of nineteen. If a writer doesn't care enough about his work to paint *precisely* the right picture, why should the reader waste his time reading it?

Conversely, a work devoid of comparison may also be problematic; sometimes a clearer picture needs to be drawn, especially of an obscure idea. A manuscript bereft of comparison usually ends up registering with the reader intellectually but not emotionally; he may understand it perfectly well but still mysteriously put it down, for some unnameable reason not feeling *compelled* to turn its pages. On the other hand, a manuscript filled to the brim with comparison—even if apt—may be so overwrought, so laboured, that in its whirlwind of ideas, it prevents the reader from grasping any ideas at all.

Solutions

The good news is that poor comparisons are easy to identify, if not from your perspective, then at least from a (good) outside reader's. As with most writing maladies, identification is half the battle: once you know what you're dealing with, you can at the very least remove it. Replacing it, or coming up with better comparisons, is harder, but it can be done with time, and the exercises at the end of this chapter should help in this regard.

For the Manuscript Overusing Comparison

- Comparison is a major tool, not to be used lightly or frequently. The first step is to determine whether you were right in using it at all. Is the idea at hand really clouded (or significant) enough to warrant a comparison (remember, the reader is smarter than you think), or are you just using it because it popped into your head and sounded nice? Has comparison already been used in close proximity? (Within one page is 'close'.) If the answer to the first question is no and the second yes, then you probably should not be using the comparison to begin with. Take it out.

- If you are firm in your conviction that comparison must be used, the next step is to see if your comparison is commonplace or clichéd (such as 'They dropped like flies', or 'He was sweating like a pig'). If you are honestly self-scrutinizing, this is something you should be able to determine yourself. If so, take it out.

- If you have determined both that the comparison is necessary and that it is not clichéd, then the final check is to see if it illuminates the idea at hand with utmost precision. For this, you can be self-scrutinizing, but it won't always work. It is probably best to call in objective readers. Just as there is a

world of difference between a word that is *right* and a word
that is *perfect*, there is likewise a world of difference between a
comparison that works and a comparison that brings the reader
to a new level of enlightenment.

For the Manuscript Devoid of Comparison

It is unusual for a reader to come across a spot in a manuscript and
say, 'I really wish there were a comparison here.' The mind doesn't
work that way: it will find awkward comparisons easily, but won't
necessarily look for places to insert good ones. Thus, determining
that you actually need comparison can be difficult. The easiest way to
make the determination is if a specific passage or concept is difficult
to understand, if it somehow hasn't drawn a crystal clear picture in
your mind. This is commonly the case with character description:
you can describe a character's face for pages on end and still not draw
a clear picture, or you can say, 'He looked like John Travolta' and
nothing more need be said. The task is done in five words.

The other, harder, way of determining if a manuscript can use
comparison is if, by the end, it has a general 'bland' feeling: it's
not bad, but it's not spectacular either. Perhaps comparison is one
of the tools that can be used to help 'spice it up'.

Examples

*John ran down the block **like a banshee**. He was sweating **like a
pig**. He checked in to see his Aunt Shirley, who looked **as pale as a
ghost**. She served him a drink which tasted **as sour as a lemon**. He
went outside and lay **like a blanket** on the grass. Pretty soon, **night
fell like a curtain**, and he was **cold as an icicle**. He **shivered like
a snowman** and got up and **hobbled home like a cripple**. His teeth
were **chattering like a skeleton's**. He went into his own house and*

*was **as hungry as a bear**. He **chastised his wife as if she were a little girl** because the food was as **hot as a fire**. He then started **laughing like a madman** and she knew he was as **crazy as a loon**.*

One of the things you'll notice about comparison is that it *slows down* a text, This is why comparison comes hand in hand with pacing (see Chapter 19, 'Pacing and Progression') and why the more experienced writer must take this into account when deciding whether to use comparison. For instance, occasionally you'll come across an apt comparison but it will still need to be cut because it interferes with the pacing of a culminating paragraph or chapter. Sometimes you'll have to decide what's more important—getting the comparison across, or ending the chapter (or paragraph) with a bang?

In the above example, you get an idea of the cumulative effect of clichéd comparisons. You'll probably scoff at this example and say, 'Mine's not that bad; I have nothing to worry about.' But you do. The effect is exaggerated here, but if you have even one commonplace comparison, you bring a portion of this distasteful effect into your manuscript. And distasteful effects—even minute ones—accumulate quickly over the course of two, three, or four hundred pages.

*Amy thought Sara was as **ugly as a cucumber**. She remembered her in first grade, when she was as **smart as a bullet,** but now she was not bright at all; rather, she was **dull as a lamp**. She wondered why she followed her around **as if she were a treasurer**. She wished Sara would stop calling her, **pestering her like a rodent**. She hated her calls, dreaded their coming **like a bad movie**. Sara was trying to torture her **like a magician**. But she had had enough and would tell her so. She would **speak her mind like a princess** and tell her never to call again. She wished she had never known her, had just **forgotten about her like a bad memory**. But she was doomed to be **plagued like a prisoner**.*

Here we have examples of mismatched comparison; none of the above is quite right. How ugly is a cucumber? How smart is a bullet? How dull is a lamp? At first glance these comparisons may sound right, but a lamp is actually not dull at all—in fact, it is bright. A lamp *shade* perhaps, is dull, but even not necessarily that. This writer is close, but still off. For instance, she wouldn't follow her around as if she were a 'treasurer', but as if she were a 'leader'. She wouldn't pester her like a 'rodent', but like a 'gnat' or a 'fly'. This raises another issue, which is *specificity* in writing.

Specificity

Minor distinctions can make a major difference. Specificity is what distinguishes poor from good from brilliant writing. As a writer, you must train your mind to be, above all, *exacting*. Make distinctions upon distinctions. Don't rest until you have exactly the right word.

This may demand you do some research: if so, check a dictionary or thesaurus, ask an expert. If you are writing a medical thriller, find out the exact names of medical instruments—speak to doctors, go to a hospital and examine the instruments yourself. Instead of saying 'insects hit the windscreen', name the insects; instead of saying 'birds flew overhead', name the birds. This is what lends authenticity to a manuscript, what brings it to life, what makes it *real*. It will be so specific, the reader will think, 'He can't be making this up.' Readers will not only be impressed, but they'll feel as if they're entering a world they immediately recognize, as if they're learning something new, be it the name of a bird, insects, or tree they've never heard before. We must remember that reading is as much about education as it is entertainment, and even small flourishes can help serve this function and add a whole new dimension to a text.

Vocabulary

Similarly, extended vocabulary—if properly used—is impressive. It is rare to come across unusual words in manuscripts these days. It is as if all of today's writers were working from a secondary school-level vocabulary—and writers who do use unusual words more often than not misuse them. I'm not saying you should learn big words to impress readers; I'm saying you should learn big words to increase your arsenal as a writer. If good writing is about finding the precise word, what greater aid to this could there be than having many at your disposal? A benefit is that you'll cut down the sheer number of words in your manuscript, because when you really have the right one, you can stop dancing around the definition. For instance, you could say, 'They landed on the beach and stopped before the pile of rocks that looked like it had been erected as some sort of marker', or 'They landed on the beach and stopped before the *cairn*'.

When you begin to learn a foreign language, if you try thinking or talking in that language, you'll find you can only construct limited sentences, using basic words. But the more you increase your vocabulary in that language, the more far-reaching your *thoughts* can be. The same holds true for English. If you know only basic words, you can only construct basic sentences—after all, what are sentences but compilations of words? The fact is, the vast majority of us do know only basic words, considering that we know only a fraction of the words in our dictionary. Most of us stop actively trying to increase our vocabulary after secondary school or university. This is a huge mistake, particularly for writers.

Words are the tools of writers. Not having the best ones at your fingertips is like a mechanic not having the best tools in his toolbox; knowing words but not knowing how to use them is like a mechanic having the tools but not knowing what to do with them. If you are a serious writer, you have an obligation never to stop actively learning words. If you have slacked off in this regard, the time to start again is now. Here are three things you can do. (1) Go out and buy a box of five hundred or a thousand index cards (preferably with vocabulary words preprinted on them, definitions on the back). If you can't find these, buy blank index cards and inscribe them with words you don't know, the word on one side, the definition on the other. Start by learning three or five words a day. Don't try to learn more than five a day, or you will end up not remembering any. Or, if you prefer, you can buy one of the many books devoted to increasing vocabulary which can be found on the market today. (2) From now on, when you come across a word you don't know in your reading (any reading), mark it, come back to it, make an index card for it, and add it to your box of words. (3) From now on, when you come across a word you don't know in conversation, stop its user and ask its meaning. It may be embarrassing, especially because people tend to cut other people down for not knowing a word, but that's their problem, not yours. At the end of the day, you are the one who walks away with the extra word. As you extend your vocabulary, you'll soon find yourself *thinking* in broader terms. And when you reach the next impasse in your writing, groping for that right word—suddenly, like that, you'll know it.

A word of caution: it's great to learn new words, but your playground should be speech and writing exercises, not your actual manuscript. Great painters don't experiment with colours or brushes they're unfamiliar with in the midst of their great works; musicians won't throw in a foreign chord in the midst of a carefully orchestrated piece. Likewise, never use a word in your writing you are not first intimately familiar with, that you do not use routinely in real life. Otherwise, it will immediately ring false. When you suspect a word you've used sounds wrong, or is a stretch, often it is; ask yourself if you would have used it in speech. Often the answer will be no, and you should thus take it out.

Simplicity, as in other elements of writing, still reigns supreme: extended vocabulary is not synonymous with extended-syllable words. On the contrary, the writer who holds the dictionary in his head will often opt for a word of surprising brevity.

To know a word, you should learn not only its definition but its pronunciation (and variations)—are you going to get up on stage and mispronounce words you've written? To know a word intimately you should also know its past usage, if different, and its root, origin, history. This sounds like a lot, but paradoxically, it will increase your chances of retaining it, as these associations will ground it for you. To make it your own, use it not only in speech, but in your thoughts. After several weeks of usage, it will be a word you can use fluently. Then, and only then, may you use it in your writing.

> *The man had a long, drawn-out face. He was very pale. His forehead ran straight across. He had large, dark circles beneath his eyes and a long scar running beneath his neck. The scar was badly stitched, so the needle and thread marks were actually still apparent. He was very tall and very broad and he had a deathly pallor to him. He was slow of movement and badly coordinated. He didn't know his own strength. He didn't seem very bright. He had a very deep voice. He moaned a lot. He stumbled around. His clothes were ragged and torn.*

To say a manuscript actually *needs* comparison is always subjective. But look at the above example. The writer can say all this, or he might simply say, 'The man looked like Frankenstein.' Which is easier?

Let's look at some comparisons that *do* work:

> *It was as though the trees around the house had been planted by fire. Their branches were twisted with crippled black arms*

and tropical berries that looked poisonous under waxed flowers. Italian cypress, so easy to grow in Los Angeles, stuck out in neat rows, wind bent at vulgar angles and hiding things that flew. Its hedges were voluptuous as an old French bed, pulsing with fat roses that spilled over a short front lawn of pink and white gravel.

Donald Rawley, *Slow Dance on the Fault Line*

Notice Rawley's unusual images: 'planted by fire'; the branches' 'crippled black arms'; comparing the hedges to 'an old French bed'. He exhibits skill in other ways, too—berries that 'looked poisonous'; the unusual adjective 'waxed' for flowers; the specific naming of 'Italian cypress' and the description of 'wind bent at vulgar angles' that modifies the cypress, as well as the strange and deliberately vague idea that they were 'hiding things that flew'. All in four sentences.

Another effective usage of comparison can be found in Fyodor Dostoevsky's *Notes from Underground*: 'I'm suspicious and easily offended, like a dwarf or a hunchback.' Anyone can say they're 'suspicious and easily offended' and the reader will grasp this intellectually, but adding 'like a dwarf or a hunchback' makes the reader understand not just intellectually, but emotionally. In *Moby-Dick*, Herman Melville says: 'Methinks that in looking at things spiritual, we are too much like oysters observing the sun through the water, and thinking that thick water the thinnest of air.' This is more potent than just saying, 'We think we know more than we do about spiritual matters.' It also draws a picture we will not forget, one of light and water, evocative of spirituality itself.

End-of-Chapter Exercises

Teaching someone to come up with good comparisons is among the most difficult things in writing; comparisons, more than any element of writing, draw on vision. But here are a few exercises that should at least make you aware of and acclimatize you to the process, and hopefully help stimulate imagination.

- Take an object in your room and come up with ten comparisons for it. For the first five comparisons, use similes; for the next five, use metaphors. For instance, 'The dresser, tall and narrow, looked like an upright coffin'; and then 'The dresser, tall and narrow, was an altar.' Don't let yourself use clichéd comparisons, and make sure each one is truly enlightening, teaching us something we don't already know about the object.

- Now come up with ten comparisons (similes and metaphors) to describe the action that same object is taking. For instance, 'The dresser leaned against the wall like a bored security guard'; and then 'The dresser, leaning against the wall, was an abandoned baseball bat.'

- Now do the same exercise, but instead of an object, use a person. Do it again for a person's characteristics, his demeanour, his mood. Then do the exercise for settings in general, for moods in general. Finally, do the exercise for anything at all in your manuscript that you've been wanting to describe with greater precision, anywhere you feel you haven't quite said all you wanted to say, or anywhere you had a strong visual image in mind and didn't quite convey it.

5

Style

The advances for my last eight books have been, in the order I received them: eighteen, fifteen, twenty, twenty, seven, twenty-five, three, twenty, and eight thousand dollars. Some of these books have earned additional royalties, and some haven't. These modest numbers do not generate much excitement among agents, editors, or writers with stars in their eyes, but they are real numbers earned by a working writer. They are real advances for real books in the real world.

Eric Maisel, *Deep Writing*

STYLE can be the downfall of many otherwise talented writers. Style can be too archaic (often found with the historical writer), too florid (the romance writer), too minimalist (the trendy writer), too academic (the professor), or too clipped or too protracted (the less talented experimentalist), to name but a few common problems. All of these writers think they add a distinctive flavour, a 'richness', to the text, but more often than not they are just indulging themselves—thus the term 'self-indulgent'—a common symptom of the overstyled manuscript.

Of course, there are times when a certain amount of style, of flair, is appropriate, even welcome—even *necessary*—such as when used as an adjunct to a viewpoint or as a propellant to the beginning or end of a chapter (see Chapter 14, 'Hooks'). For instance, if you are writing a novel told from the first-person viewpoint of a deranged man, you'd probably want the prose to be fragmented or in some other way noticeably different, in keeping with this narrator's way of seeing the world—indeed, in this case the prose would *have* to be heavily styled, or else risk being inauthentic. Incidentally, this is the primary reason why every book on writing warns beginners to stay away from first-person narration, to stay away from narrators that demand a certain degree of style—and for good reason: this type of narration, of style, is the hardest to pull off, even for the most advanced writer. It requires building a delicate facade and maintaining it without the slightest deviation (and without being monotonous, annoying, or distracting the reader) for the entire length of the work. Even one tiny break, one word out of keeping, and the facade will come crumbling down.

When handled well, style can add a new dimension to a text, give it a certain 'feel' that nothing else can, give it an unnameable charm; when handled expertly, it can go so far as to advance the overall message of the text. Think of the minimalism of the existentialists, the plaintive simplicity of *The Stranger*'s narration and how it furthers the message of its narrator; or the mysterious quietness of *The Castle*'s style and how it complements the surreal, snow-dampened town; or the relentless style of *Absalom, Absalom!* and how it complements its subject, a crumbling, strife-torn Southern family littered, like the book's endlessly long sentences, with secrets calling to be unearthed.

But most of the time, in the present day, in the vast majority of unsolicited manuscripts, style is misused. It is one of the easiest things to spot, even for the lay reader, and subsequently one of the easiest ways to dismiss a manuscript.

A few ways to tell if a manuscript suffers from stylistic errors:

1. The writing feels forced or exaggerated, as if it doesn't quite fit its subject.
2. The writing seems to be not so much about the story or characters as about the writing itself, as if the entire book were merely an arena for the writer to exhibit his talent.

3. The writing is too noticeable; it keeps getting in the *way*. It reaches a point where it even impedes your getting involved in the story.
4. Redundancy. Events and ideas keep repeating themselves with only a slightly different twist.
5. Ultimately, you feel as if you're being used as a reader, it becoming apparent that the writing is not meant for you but for the writer himself.

Solutions

Stylistic errors are among the easiest to recognize and the hardest to fix. Even dubbing a style 'wrong' can be called into question, because style is, after all, subjective. But when you have a consensus from several apt readers that your style is seriously impeding their involvement in the text, then you know you have a problem that needs to be addressed.

A stylistic problem is a whole different animal from, say, an adjective or adverb problem, which, as we saw previously, can be easily fixed. In most instances, you'll probably end up having to discard your style altogether and start over again. But even if this is the case, even if after scrutinizing your style problem you are only able to conclude that you do indeed *have* one—and if you are willing to start again—then you've achieved your main objective. Additionally, you'll be able to keep in mind the principles you've learned in recognizing your poor style and at least have some idea of what to avoid in your new one.

Style is like a beast lurking beneath the text, always wanting to break out, always needing to be kept at bay. If you (and others) conclude that your style is good but has just got out of hand in places (as it tends to do, even for the best of writers) then there are some ways you can tame the beast.

A few practical solutions for the overeager stylist:

- Take a step back and ask yourself what's more important: your writing or the story? Would you rather readers admire your writing, or become engrossed? If you answer the former, you must change your way of thinking. You must realize that when a reader gets lost in your story, turns pages rapidly, and does *not* notice your writing, he is paying you the highest compliment. Unfortunately, these days, 'literary' writing seems to have become synonymous with 'showy' writing, writing that is beautiful but doesn't tell a story. This is a misguided trend. If today's 'literary' writers would look back only one or two hundred years at real literary writers like Dostoevsky, Poe, Conrad, Melville, they would find momentous stories—not just pretty writing—at the core of almost all their great works.

- Ask yourself if your style is genuinely appropriate for the story, if it is in line with its intention. *A style should complement a story, not fight against it.* Like a slave, it should always serve the story and never itself.

- How would your style be different if, instead of putting ink to paper, you told your story aloud to friends? (Start right now, tell it to the air; notice carefully how and where you differ from what's written.) Your telling is probably more casual, more straightforward. Can any of these changes be incorporated to help relax your style, make it less studied?

- Now that we've grappled with some general, more philosophic solutions, let's get into specifics: at the risk of sounding obvious, if your sentences are too long, shorten them, break them into several sentences, use semicolons and dashes. If they're too short, lengthen them, combine them, again using semicolons and dashes. If your style is archaic, take out the convolutions, the anachronistic flourishes (like the double negative), and infuse a more modern feel (short sentences, contractions, intimate narration) to help balance it out. If it is too florid, make it more straightforward; if too minimal, embellish it, throw in some analogies, more description, more feeling.

- The academic style is an issue in and of itself. It is perhaps the most commonly encountered form of stylistic error, for professors (and graduate students—frequently with theses) often try to break into mainstream publishing. Style is inevitably their obstacle. (Indeed, when an agent or editor sees a manuscript is by a professor, he automatically assumes it's going to be too academic.) Even university presses, with their recent push into the general market, are trying to get away from the overly academic book. The problem with academics is threefold: (1) they are overly argumentative—they approach a book as if it were a long argument, an essay, a paper; (2) their prose is unnecessarily convoluted—they often look for the most roundabout way of expressing an idea; (3) their foremost concerns are accuracy and thoroughness, whereas the foremost concern of a trade writer is keeping the reader engrossed. Academics often stuff their manuscripts with abundant, unnecessary references and parenthetical citations. But what good are all these references if nobody can read past the first page? The solutions to these three problems, now that we've dissected them, should be self-evident.

- Once you feel you've smoothed out your style problem, go through your manuscript one more time and check for redundancy, for places where you might have repeated an event or idea with only a slightly new twist. Cut them. If the *purpose* of your book is to convey one event from several different perspectives (as in, for instance, *Twelve Angry Men*), then it's okay; otherwise, you should be able to do it the first time.

Examples

The boy ran. Into the woods. It was dark. Scary. The light pulsed through the leaves. It started to rain. Cold. He fell. He got up. He ran again. His pursuer was right behind. He heard him. Breathing. He tripped. He got up. He tripped again. He banged into a tree. Pain. In his arm. It stung. The pursuer. Catching up. He couldn't go on. The boy. He hid. Behind a tree. He heard him coming. He didn't move. Couldn't. Wouldn't. He waited. He passed. Or so he thought. He came back ...

A good example of a novice experimentalist trying to add what he probably thinks is heightened effect or suspense to his prose (don't laugh, I've seen examples much worse than this—where it kept up for three hundred pages). But what is the result? The writing draws attention to itself, making it extremely difficult to focus on the events at hand. An example like this—a blatant case of a disastrous style—is the most easily fixed. Sentences can be combined; repetition can be cut. When the writer really wants the dramatic effect of a short sentence, he can use it once or twice (probably close to the end of a paragraph or chapter).

Remember: writing is about *contrast*. If all sentences are short, the effect is lost. Nothing stands out. But if many sentences are long (or at least of medium length), and then a short sentence comes along, that sentence will have the desired effect. This is also one of the ways to add meaning to a sentence without hitting the reader over the head; the brevity will resonate with the reader in a more subtle, refined way.

The Roman Empire of Caligula, as referenced by Mr Hawkins, in his treatise, The Political Climate of Pre-Napoleonic Europe and Its Early Roots in the Roman Empire, *might indeed be seen as something, even to that most hardened sceptic, of a mystery, that is, an enigma, in, of course, the larger sense of the word. The internal structure of the bureaucracy, as witnessed by Chief Councillor Spiros Andros and documented by Epilos, was not unlike the Cartesian dynasty of the 6th century, under the little-known Habacus of Southern France (ibid., p.899), not in its want of a political head, that is to say, a leader, but rather in its seeming tolerance and perhaps even inclination towards that one desire man has been struggling to conquer since the earliest days of Scripture. We might find a parallel here to the late Napoleon, not to him, per se, but to his third man, Bijeuax, as mentioned by the of course impartial H. Ringeus, writing in what might be termed his late-Victorian monograph,* The Infusion of Normandy and Its Effect on the Demographic of the Northern European, Most Particularly the Rural Dweller.

What is he talking about?! This sort of academic style will sooner or later make you want to pull your hair out. Looking closely, you'll see all the classic signs of the academic: the plethora of qualifiers and references (terrified of potential criticism, the academic will never just come out and say something without first either guarding his statements, qualifying them in some way, or referencing someone else) and also an extreme reluctance to get to the point! Academics seem to take joy in dancing around an issue (sometimes for pages at a time). Finally, the sentences are long and convoluted and go off on endless tangents, making one wonder if the academic ever looks twice at his work before sending it to the printer.

I couldn't help thinking as I walked out of the doctor's office if I'd ever see him again if I'd done the right thing by coming in the first place and I felt so bad for racking up all these bills and knew I had no right when Billy was in the hospital but I just couldn't help it and then it started to rain and I couldn't help wondering

*if that was a sign too the rain and all if it was a sign that maybe
I'd done something wrong something terribly terribly wrong like
I'd done my whole life. You know how sometimes these things just
creep up on you when you're thinking and all you can do is think
think think like the time I was a little girl and was playing with
Matty in the park and there were all these clouds and I'd see the
shapes in them and they'd just keep going and going ....*

Here we have the so-called stream of consciousness being employed
by the stylist who likes to come up for air maybe once a page. This
is how we feel as readers, too: gasping. It is impossible to focus
on content when sentences are expanded in such a way; it might
sound pretty to the writer, but it's not doing him any good.

End-of-Chapter Exercises

There is no recipe for a perfect style because style, more than
most aspects of writing, is based on inspiration. But the following
exercises should help you explore the possibilities.

- Temporarily let go of your style (you can always bring it back if
  you don't like the change) and try just telling your story in as
  straightforward a manner as possible. This usually breeds a new,
  natural style that is more in line with the text, with facilitating the
  narration of the story. Telling your story aloud, as discussed in
  the solutions on p. 55, will help in this regard.
- Try using the exact opposite style. If your style is straightforward, try one that is convoluted; if it is baroque, try one
  that is minimalist. Even if you don't end up using the new
  style, some very interesting changes may arise that can be
  incorporated in the final text. These will help balance it, add
  moments of contrast.

- If you are having a hard time (as most of us do) figuring out the style that would be most in line with the intention of your text, one of the things you can do is look to the *dialogue* of your viewpoint narrator. The idea behind this is, because he is narrating the text, the way he speaks—tough, effeminate, terse, windy—will in most cases be the appropriate way to flavour the narration (particularly with first-person narration). There can be exceptions, used, say, for droll effect: the narrator who puts on airs of being street tough in relating the story to us (the readers) but whose dialogue is actually cowardly (or vice versa), or the narrator who is effusive when speaking to us (the readers) but reserved in his dialogue. It is realistic for there to be some discrepancy between a character's thoughts (narration) and words (dialogue). As in real life, he might think one thing and say another for many reasons: out of intentional deceit, out of sheer nervousness, out of a momentary inability to phrase his thoughts. Barring this, however, there should probably be a close parallel between the viewpoint character's dialogue and his narration (particularly the style of his narration), so if you find his dialogue comes easily but are stuck as to style, try letting his dialogue flavour it.

Part II
Dialogue

Oₙ our path to rejecting the manuscript, dialogue should, in truth, come first, as dialogue reveals the skill of a writer instantaneously. It comes second in this book, though, because, despite its being a quick determinant, dialogue is generally looked at second by publishing professionals, for confirmation. If, at a quick glance, our initial impression of a manuscript is that it suffers from one of the preliminary problems, we then look to the dialogue: if it, too, is poor, we needn't look any further. In this way, an evaluation of a five-hundred-page manuscript can sometimes take less than five seconds. And it is accurate 99 per cent of the time.

Dialogue reflects sensibility. A book with little or no dialogue might be called 'quiet'; conversely, a book filled to the brim with dialogue might be called 'loud'. A book that hurls us into dialogue from the first line might be called 'impatient', while one that takes its time before releasing the first word might be called 'controlled'.

Dialogue is a powerful tool, to be used sparingly, effectively, and at the right moment. Dialogue is to the writer what the veto is to the president: it gives you great power and authority. If you overuse it, people will have to submit, but they will resent you for it; if you use it wisely, they will applaud your control, your willpower.

Dialogue is prey to a thousand possible ailments. In Part II, we'll cover five of the most common, one chapter devoted to each.

6

Between the Lines

Despite popular misconception, most agents and editors don't read in the office. They read during nights and weekends, *after* work, *after* ten- or twelve-hour days. Most agents and editors receive 500 or more manuscripts a month, or about twenty a day. Now you might understand why they'll become savage if you pressure them to read your manuscript in any amount of time. Why should they? The average entry-level salary for an editorial assistant is roughly £11,000 a year. With no pay, with reading demanded on leisure time, book publishing is as high pressured as Hollywood, with few of the perks. And in publishing you *really* have to read—not 120-page screenplays, but often 300-, 400-, or 500-page novels. This is why book publishing is one of the highest burn-out industries. This is why there's something called the 'two-year mark' in publishing, that is, why most who enter it end up leaving by their two-year mark.

WHAT'S most interesting about dialogue is that you can dismiss it without even reading it. Instead, just look at its *appearance* on the page. For instance, if I skim through a manuscript and see pages and pages filled with dialogue, with no breaks or rests in between, chances are it's going to be rejected. Conversely, if I skim through dozens of pages and find not one line of dialogue, chances are it's going to be rejected too. These examples are but a couple of a whole slew of maladies that can come *between the lines* of dialogue, that can get your manuscript dismissed without an agent or editor even looking at the words. Four of the more common one are:

1. Identifiers (also known as 'attributives'). Identifiers—such as 'he said'—are not an issue for playwrights or screenwriters, who, in their craft, simply need to centre the speaker's name and then insert the lines of dialogue beneath it. But when it comes to the novel, this issue suddenly arises. How many times do you have to keep saying 'he said'? When should you use 'he' and when the character's name? Should you use 'he said' or 'said he'? Do you place these identifiers at the beginning, middle, or end of what's spoken? Errors in any of these respects can signal an amateur. There are other potential problems with identifiers, including their absence, their adversely affecting rhythm and pacing, and the (more rare) absence of quotation marks and use of paraphrasing.

2. Spitfire dialogue. Some writers fill their manuscripts with long interchanges of dialogue without any pauses in between. It's as if they're in a rush to get through the book. This sort of dialogue can be spotted without even looking at the words, and is usually cause for immediate dismissal. Playwrights and screenwriters-turned-novelists fall prey to this because they're used to listing their dialogue down the page, separated only by the speakers' names. They're used to including in their scripts only the barest stage direction—the rest they leave up to directors and actors. But imagine if directors and actors didn't fill this in. Imagine what a play or film would be like if the actors just stood there, rooted in one spot, and delivered lines back and forth to one another without moving at all. This is the effect that this type of dialogue has on the reader of the novel. Dialogue must be broken up, stretched out, not just with identifiers, but with pauses, breaks, direction; otherwise

the pace accelerates too quickly (see Chapter 19, 'Pacing and Progression'). When it comes to the written word, there are no actors and directors who are going to do it for you—what you see is what you get.

3. Dialogue interrupted. On the flip side, you find dialogue that needs to flow but is either interrupted by long breaks of description, or is continually interrupted by shorter spates of identifiers and modifiers. This is more rare, but when it does happen, it can not only become annoying but also ruin the rhythm, pacing, and momentum, especially in the midst of a heated interchange.

4. Journalistic dialogue. As the name implies, this malady often affects the work of magazine or newspaper journalists trying to make the switch to fiction. They tend to quote their characters instead of letting their dialogue flow in fully-fledged scenes. This ends up giving the text a factual, reportorial feel, as if the characters' dialogue is merely being used to reinforce a point. This type of dialogue is often spotted in the middle of paragraphs, instead of initiating a paragraph as it rightly should.

Solutions

• Identifiers should do their job—let us know who's speaking—as quietly as possible, without drawing attention to themselves or getting in the way. When a person first speaks, you should use his name to identify him, but afterwards you may simply use 'he'. If there are multiple parties speaking, you may need to continually identify people by their names, but whenever possible it is preferable to simply use the appropriate pronoun. Continually using someone's name becomes repetitive and will eventually ring discordantly in the reader's ear. Repeatedly using 'he' will also eventually become stale (though tolerance is greater), and to avoid this the writer should, whenever possible, use no identifier at all. (As is always the case in writing, it is preferable to use as few words as we can.) This will be most likely to work if there are few parties present and if the reader is intimately familiar with who is speaking.

If identifiers are absent altogether—usually done as a stylistic statement—this will inevitably lead to confusion and is almost always cause for rejection. Occasionally some writers use identifiers but will not use quotation marks, will not offset their dialogue (again, a stylistic statement), but this almost always fails and I would not recommend it, especially for beginning writers. Generally, any writer who employs this is more interested in calling attention to the writing itself instead of to what's being said. A third variation on the absence of identifiers is the use of paraphrasing. This has its place, but again should only be used sparingly.

Most writers opt for 'he said' instead of 'said he'. Both are acceptable, although the latter can be archaic and awkward. A reader will eventually get used to anything, so if you insist on using the latter, it's not a tragedy, but don't switch frequently between the two. Some writers alternate every other line with 'said he' and 'he said', presumably for variety, but manuscripts like these just make for awkward reading and are immediately rejected.

Identifiers are traditionally placed after what's said. They can sometimes be found at the beginning or in the middle, but this is usually done for effect. Note the difference:

'Do you love me?' she asked.
'Do you,' she asked, 'love me?'

The latter clearly draws more attention to itself, also implying a pause in the midst of the phrase. This is okay, but again, only if used sparingly. If a writer is constantly switching his identifiers from the beginning to the middle to the end, this will inevitably lead to distraction.

As my editor so keenly reminded me, it needn't always be 'said', either; for variation, one can replace 'said' with verbs like 'yelled', 'cried', 'whispered', 'groaned', 'hissed'. Additionally, you can describe the *way* your character said something, as in 'he said, his eyes narrowing' or 'he said, his voice dripping with sarcasm'. You can even link an action to the identifier, as in 'he said, pulling cocaine from his gym bag' or 'he said, stabbing the elevator button repeatedly'. Of the three options, this last is most preferable, but I would strongly advise, especially beginning writers, to use extreme caution when replacing 'said'. Associating actions with the word can add a nice layer of subtext, but replacing it with other verbs is hard to pull off well and often leans too far toward telling (see Chapter 11, 'Showing Versus Telling').

• Dialogue is inherently dramatic, and many writers work themselves up in order to get a scene flowing. Subsequently, many writers, once they begin dialogue, have a hard time stopping, seem to feel the need to do a long spate at once. These writers must learn to restrain themselves, to sustain suspense and to let a scene unfold slowly. They must learn to appreciate the effect dialogue has on pacing (see Chapter 19, 'Pacing and Progression') and must temper their interchanges with pauses, breaks, and action, to give the reader time to absorb it. They must learn control, the value of silence, learn how to stretch a scene for pages at a time with only a few lines of dialogue.

• Conversely, those who tend to interrupt their dialogue (more rare) with endless identifiers or excessive description must learn to let it flow, to let scenes happen. This especially holds true for high moments of anger, when heated interchanges need to unfold with urgency. One function of dialogue is to allow a break in the monotony of description; dialogue continually interrupted will not allow this break, but will rather just end up frustrating the reader further.

- The journalistic writers who quote their characters need to learn that their characters aren't there to reinforce the writer's points but to raise their own voices. Characters are not to be quoted, but to speak for themselves. These writers should practise moving their dialogue to the beginning of paragraphs and take to heart that dialogue is not to be employed lightly, that when it does come, it should often merit a fully-fledged scene.

Examples

'Hey Paul, how ya doin'?' John said.
'Just fine, John, how about you?' Paul said.
'Okay, Paul,' John said.
'That's good, John,' Paul said.
He said, 'What do you think of that car?'
He answered, 'I think it's nice.'
'I think,' he said, 'it's nice, too.'
'Well I think that,' he said, 'that's good.'
'Well, I'm glad,' said he.
'I am too,' said he.
He said he thought they should leave now.
He agreed that they should.

Here's an example of how identifiers, when poorly used, can really distract the reader (or at least make for awkward reading). Note the unnecessary repetition of the name 'John' in the identifier in line 3. Only John and Paul are talking, so when John says, 'Okay, Paul', we know it must be John who's saying this; likewise with the repetition of 'Paul' in line 4. Note the placement of the identifiers at the beginning in lines 5 and 6 and then in the middle in 7 and 8; the writer thinks he's adding variety, but he's actually just distracting us. In lines 9 and 10, note the awkward usage of 'said he', and in the final two lines, note the awkward usage of paraphrasing. Any of these identifiers might work by themselves, but when mixed, they just distract.

'Stop! Police!'
'Hey man, I didn't do nothing.'
'Don't move! You're under arrest!'
'Hey man, it's not me!'
'Shut up! Up against the wall!'
'Ow, you're hurting me!'
'Now get in the car!'
'Ow, my head!'
'Don't say a word until we get to the station!'
'Are we there yet?'
'Okay, out of the car. We're here.'

Here's some non-stop dialogue for you. You'll notice it feels as if it is moving too fast, as if it needs something to slow it down and let you take in what's happening. In cases like this, the writing moves so fast that it doesn't feel real to the reader, prevents him from truly getting involved in the text. It's also difficult to follow the action, as the dialogue is trying to do all the work.

It was very cold outside. They were all aware of how cold it was. They were bundled up in their clothes. When asked what she thought of the weather, Jane said, 'It's very cold out. My feet are freezing.'

John untied the sled dogs and got everyone settled on the sled. They all got seated and were ready to go. John was sweating and looked tired from the effort. When Jane asked him what he thought of the job, he said, 'It's hard work.'

Note the journalistic feel when the characters are quoted at the end of each paragraph; it feels as if they're being used to make a point. And their quotes, since they're mostly used for emphasis, also end up being repetitive.

Here, however, is an example of dialogue that does work. This is taken from Albert Camus's *The Stranger*:

> *That evening Marie came by to see me and asked me if I wanted to marry her. I said it didn't make any difference to me and that we could if she wanted to. Then she wanted to know if I loved her. I answered the same way I had the last time, that it didn't mean anything but that I probably didn't love her. 'So why marry me, then?' she said. I explained to her that it didn't really matter and that if she wanted to, we could get married. Besides, she was the one who was doing the asking and all I was saying was yes. Then she pointed out that marriage was a serious thing. I said, 'No.' She stopped talking for a minute and looked at me without saying anything. Then she spoke. She just wanted to know if I would have accepted the same proposal from another woman, with whom I was involved in the same way. I said, 'Sure.' Then she said she wondered if she loved me, and there was no way I could know about that. After another moment's silence, she mumbled that I was peculiar, that that was probably why she loved me but that one day I might hate her for the same reason. I didn't say anything because I didn't have anything to add, so she took my arm with a smile and said she wanted to marry me ....*

Note how in this entire example the only lines of dialogue are 'So why marry me, then?', 'No', and 'Sure'. It feels as if there were more, doesn't it? The reason Camus is able to get away with this is because he uses the space between the lines of dialogue to set us up; he doesn't use the dialogue for his own ends, to convey information (see Chapter 8, 'Informative'). He also uses some advanced, unusual techniques here, such as not offsetting the dialogue but letting it run continuously in the paragraph, paraphrasing his characters, and contrasting minimal dialogue with longer sentences. The effect is that we feel the reticence of the protagonist.

End-of-Chapter Exercises

- For those of you who tend to plough forward with dialogue without stopping for breaks, practise the following: take a scene from your manuscript and rewrite it using only half the lines of dialogue and stretching it twice as long. For instance, if your original scene had ten lines of dialogue and spanned one page, your new scene will have five lines of dialogue and span two pages. You will be pressed to figure out ways of filling in the gaps. Can any of these be incorporated in the final text?
- For those of you who stop the flow of your dialogue with too much description, practise the exact opposite: rewrite a scene from your manuscript using twice as many lines of dialogue and half the space. Allow the scene to flow by itself—stop feeling the need to control every word. Credit the reader with the ability to fill in what happens himself.

7

Commonplace

In order to even begin to learn how to play his instrument, it takes the guitarist weeks to build calluses on his fingertips; it takes the saxophonist months to strengthen his lip so that he might play his instrument for only a five-minute stretch; it can take the pianist years to develop dual hand and multiple finger coordination. Why do writers assume they can just 'write' with no training whatsoever—and then expect, on their first attempt, to be published internationally? What makes them think they're so much inherently greater, need so much less training than any other artists?

COMMONPLACE, or everyday, dialogue (such as 'Hi, how are you?' 'Fine, how are you?') is generally easy to spot and one of the most common grounds on which to dismiss a manuscript. It is analogous to the use of extraneous words like 'the' and 'that' and indicates a writer who doesn't know what to exclude, who doesn't realize how valuable the reader's time is, that he, the writer, is always in the spotlight and must never include one word not absolutely essential to the book.

Commonplace dialogue often indicates a commonplace sensibility, everyday things overheard and rehashed, a writer who is unoriginal and a manuscript that will be unoriginal. (These writers also can be spotted by the cliché.) The presence of commonplace dialogue means the manuscript as a whole will need a lot of cutting: if there is one extraneous line of dialogue on the first page, by the rule of manuscripts, you will also find one extraneous line on each page to come.

There are three major reasons why writers fall prey to using commonplace dialogue:

1. They feel the need to be 'realistic', to portray the scene as it really happened. They envisage all the greetings and niceties, and feel compelled to insert them. They fear launching (or ending) an interchange without realism, and their dialogue will usually remain painfully realistic throughout the scene.
2. Dialogue is inherently dramatic and writers sometimes need to 'work themselves up' into a scene. Sometimes they use commonplace, everyday dialogue (especially greetings and niceties and the like) to help propel them. In this case, you will usually find a discrepancy between the beginning (or end) of a scene and the rest of the dialogue. The dialogue may only be commonplace at first, righting itself once the writer settles in.
3. Finally, there is the writer with the commonplace sensibility, the writer who would prefer to rehash things from other books or films than do the work himself. This writer's main priority is usually getting his story—his 'high concept' plot—across. He doesn't really care how he gets there, doesn't care if he makes the reader stumble through four hundred pages of hackneyed prose to do it. He thinks because his plot is so great none of that other 'stuff' matters.

Solutions

Commonplace dialogue is one of the easiest things to fix. Each reason for its misusage carries its own set of solutions:

1. The urge to be 'realistic', the most common reason, must simply be resisted. Look at the narration: do you include every second

of every scene, every breath of every character, every blink of an eye, every shuffle of a foot, every beat of every heart in the room? No book could cover more than a few hours in anyone's life this way without exceeding *thousands* of pages. Realism can be conveyed in other ways. Let yourself go—I assure you, no one is going to condemn you for leaving out the 'hellos' and 'goodbyes'. On the contrary, they'll thank you for it.

2. If you use commonplace dialogue only as a propellant into (or way of tapering off) a scene, this is easily fixed. In most cases, you can just cut the everyday dialogue, and with a little smoothing out, what's left will work. All writers should be wary of this tendency: you might not write entire lines of discardable dialogue, but it is common for even the best writers to insert at least a word or two here and there, and not necessarily only at the beginning or end of a scene. A scene is a compilation of dramatic moments, and commonplace dialogue might be found throughout to help bridge these moments.

3. Dialogue that is commonplace through and through is the most difficult to fix. It cannot be cured by simple cutting; rather, this writer's entire approach to dialogue will have to be reconsidered. (For this, the exercises at the end of the chapter will be most helpful.) What this usually plot-oriented writer must realize is that, no matter how 'brilliant' his plot may be, if the road is treacherous, no one's going to want to make the journey. He must realize that, above all, in writing, the *journey* is the destination.

Examples

John slowly turned the doorknob and pushed open the door.

'Oh, hi, Mary,' he said, surprised. 'I didn't think anybody would be here.'

'Yeah,' Mary said. 'I'm working late.'

'Oh, you are?' John said. 'I didn't know. I'm sorry, I didn't mean to disturb you or anything.'

'No, it's quite all right,' Mary answered. 'I'm just typing up memos and the like.'

'Oh, that's good,' John said. 'I'm just heading to my office. In fact, I'm going to go over there now.'

'Okay, that's fine,' Mary said.

'Would you like me to bring you anything from the hall?' John asked. 'Any coffee or tea?'

'Okay,' Mary said. 'I'd like some coffee, if it's not too much trouble.'

'No,' John said. 'Not too much trouble at all. What would you like in it?'

'I'd like some milk,' Mary said. 'I'd also like some sugar if it's not too much trouble. Two packets.'

'No trouble at all,' John said. 'I'll be right back.'

'Okay, thanks a lot,' Mary said.

'Not a problem,' John answered, and walked across the room. He then opened the door and walked out and walked down the hall on his way to get Mary some coffee.

The writer who uses commonplace dialogue to be realistic can be spotted by the painstaking description preceding (or succeeding) the dialogue. He can be spotted by the 'step-by-step' feel, the determination to document every little thing that happens, in the exact order it does. Who cares how Mary takes her coffee? And after the writer goes so far as to say Mary would like milk and sugar, why go further and say 'two packets' of sugar? There are places to be specific in writing, but this is not one of them. It serves no particular purpose, in this example, such as defining a character. The case would be different if they were talking in code or referring to something between them. For instance, let's say this is the final scene of the novel, and on page 1, Mary told John that the day she took her coffee with two packets of sugar would be the day she loved him. Then the 'two packets' of sugar means everything, may even be the pivotal piece of the dialogue—of the whole book! This is one way a writer can transform something commonplace into something consequential. But context comes into play here, and without significant context, this bit of dialogue would remain insignificant. A writer must always ask himself if the details he includes further the purpose of his book. If not, he should remove them. Readers are not census takers.

> *'Hey, Jack, how ya doing?' Dave asked.*
> *'Okay, Dave, how about you?' Jack answered.*
> *'I'm all right, Jack. Listen, can I talk to you for a second?'*
> *'Sure, Dave, I'm all ears. Tell me, what's up?'*
> *'Well, I've got this story I've got to tell you,' Dave said.*
> *'Yeah? Tell me, what happened?'*
> *'I just got hit by a car.'*
> *'No!'*
> *'Yeah. I didn't even see it coming. I'm all right, now, but I must tell you something...I don't think it was an accident.'*
> *Jack just stared at him.*
> *'I think they're after me, Jack.'*

Here's an example of commonplace dialogue used as a propellant into a scene. This scene could have begun with line 7, 'I just got hit by a car'. Everything preceding it can be cut. In order to smooth out the transition, the writer could instead open the scene with a description, say, of Dave walking into Jack's office and standing there until Jack looks up. Then, after a tense moment of silence, Dave can say, 'I just got hit by a car.' Of course, there are many ways it could be improved, but here the niceties are just a precursor and actually detract from the power of the scene.

> *'Hi, John. How are you?' Mary asked.*
>
> *'Fine, Mary, how about you?' John answered.*
>
> *'Oh, I'm okay. How are things?'*
>
> *'Pretty good,' John said. 'I saw Dave the other day.'*
>
> *'Yeah?' Mary answered. 'How's he doing?'*
>
> *'Oh, he's all right,' John said. 'Same as ever. How about this weather?'*
>
> *'Yeah, how about it?' Mary asked. 'It's great, isn't it?'*
>
> *'It sure is,' John answered. 'Do you think it will hold up?'*
>
> *'Oh, I think so. I hear it's supposed to rain on Thursday, though.'*
>
> *'Yeah?' John said. 'I didn't hear that.'*
>
> *'Yeah,' Mary said. 'I heard it today on the radio. They said scattered showers.'*
>
> *'Oh,' John said. 'That's interesting. So, how are the kids?'*
>
> *'Oh, they're just fine. Thanks for asking. How about your kids?'*
>
> *'They're hanging in there. Same as usual.'*
>
> *'Oh, that's nice.'*
>
> *'Yeah, everything's fine.'*

Everything may be 'fine' in John and Mary's world, but everything's not fine with this dialogue. Here, sadly, we find the dialogue that is commonplace through and through. What can you do with writing like this? The entire passage must be cut and the approach to dialogue completely re-examined. For this, the only solution will be to work with the exercises.

End-of-Chapter Exercises

Exercises are especially helpful for dialogue problems, for which solutions are never black and white. These exercises in particular should be helpful for the writer who suffers from through-and-through commonplace dialogue.

- Ultimately, the best solution is to train your ear. Begin to pay attention to how dialogue is used in everyday life by different types of people. Eavesdrop on people—in the tube, in a cafe, walking on the street, in a shop; especially try to eavesdrop on people who might be similar to your characters. I've known some authors who've gone so far as to record conversations or take immediate notes. How does real-life dialogue differ from your characters'? You will probably find real dialogue to be clipped, bizarre, repetitive. It is often quiet—you will find many people get by with the minimum that need be said. You will probably be shocked at the discrepancy between what you hear on the street and what you've written on the page. Over time, you will fine-tune your ear and be able to draw on your experience whenever you need to.

- If you look back at your dialogue and realize you have scenes that are unsalvageable (like the last example), don't collapse in despondency. All is not lost. Instead of looking at the dialogue of the scene, look at its *set up*. Why are these characters in the room to begin with? What brings them here? Why these particular characters? What is their relationship? Where are we in the plot? How will this particular scene further the plot? By scrapping what's on the page and looking at your original *intention* for the scene, you can give yourself direction to write a new scene, one more in line with the intention of your book.

8

Informative

> Who knows why certain notes in music are capable of stirring
> the listener deeply, though the same notes slightly rearranged
> are impotent? ... There is no satisfactory explanation of style,
> no infallible guide to good writing, no assurance that a per-
> son who thinks clearly will be able to write clearly, no key that
> unlocks the door, no inflexible rule by which the young writer
> may shape his course. He will often find himself steering by stars
> that are disturbingly in motion.
>
> William Strunk and E. B. White, *The Elements of Style*

THERE are many ways in which dialogue can be 'fake'. The most common example is informative dialogue, that is, dialogue used as a vehicle for conveying information, often information that the writer is too unimaginative (or lazy) to convey in some other, more subtle way. This type of dialogue may fill the reader in on some missing facts of the plot, may provide him with a piece of information that the writer could not get across otherwise, but the price paid is great: it is dialogue that characters would never use in real life, interchanges that are not artistically real, that don't spring from characters' needs, desires, and relationships. Instead, this is dialogue imposed on them by the writer.

In real life, most dialogue is odd: clipped, repetitious, and, from an outsider's perspective, enigmatic, fragmented, filled with unknown personal references. Indeed, most genuine dialogue will, surprisingly, not tell the reader anything at all about the story. Instead, it will serve to further only the relationships between the characters—and sometimes not even that. Sometimes dialogue will provide no insights at all, just give us a glimpse into one or more characters at one moment in time. Nothing interesting may come of it, but at least it will be genuine. As a reader, you will feel as if you are in a real world, experiencing a real piece of art. This is not a pitch for realism, because the objective is that the dialogue be 'real' to whatever world you are creating, be it surreal, magic-realist, existentialist, or Kafkaesque. Indeed, on the contrary, the single biggest mistake modern-day graduate writers make is to presume that the modern-day reader is interested, above all else, in realism, interested in mundane, everyday dialogue from the East End that doesn't go anywhere or serve any greater purpose. This is a pitfall, too, but an entirely different topic, one more related to purpose and direction (which we'll touch on in Chapter 17, 'Focus').

By using dialogue to convey information, you prevent yourself from getting to the core of who your characters are, prevent interesting character dynamics, spontaneity; you stunt character growth and prevent any unusual developments that may take even *you* by surprise. The end result will be a book peopled with cardboard characters having cardboard interchanges, reading more like a prolonged synopsis than a novel. You'll never get deep enough into anything to really 'hook' the reader—indeed, readers often walk away from these novels, in the best case feeling interested but not compelled. In the worst case, this type of writing builds resentment in a reader: he'll feel cheated, as if he's read an *outline* of a story without ever getting a chance to sink his teeth into it. He's heard a story, but never became engaged by a piece of art.

Informative dialogue is most often found in 'high concept' novels, where the writer is so anxious to execute his idea that he never stops to consider the wants and needs of his characters. Dialogue of this sort is sometimes used to fill the reader in on current or future events, but is most commonly found filling the reader in on 'backstory', on things that have already happened (to this end, it is commonly found towards the beginning of manuscripts). It is also used by the writer who has not mastered the distinction between showing and telling (see Chapter 11, 'Showing Versus Telling')—whose lack of proficiency extends to his dialogue—and by the controlling writer, who maps out every last detail before he writes and refuses to let his characters grow in any way that he hasn't preplanned, who won't let them tell *him* how to run the show.

Solutions

In most cases, writers who use informative dialogue are preoccupied with story. These concept-driven writers use dialogue to serve *their* ends, and for this the best cure is to remember what we discussed in the last chapter: no matter how 'brilliant' your concept may be, if the road to your destination is not artistically real, the reader will not make the journey.

Specifically, here are some solutions for a few of the different types of plot-driven dialogue:

• Review your dialogue and ask yourself honestly if it is the natural (or real) outcome of the characters' needs, desires, relationships, or if you are just using it to get across information. If the answer is the latter, you've pinpointed problem dialogue. Take it out, but keep a note of the information you had tried to convey. Later, you can figure out how to insert it in some other way, not at the expense of dialogue.

- Take another look at the pinpointed dialogue and try to categorize it: Are you using it to convey backstory? To convey current, unfolding events? Does it arise from your need to tell instead of show? Does it come from your need to control the outcome of the scene?

- The most common malady is use of dialogue to convey backstory. The solution is to follow this rule: Dialogue should not be used to state things both characters already know, that is, one character should not remind the other character of something. It is an obvious ploy, intended only for the reader.

- If dialogue is used to convey current events, follow this rule: Don't *talk* about what's happening, *show* it. Don't have a character come running into a room and announce, 'I'm bleeding from my head'; instead, just have him come running into the room and ask for a bandage, or, even better, not say anything at all. Instead, let other characters react to the sight of him, and the reader will figure out what's happening.

- If the informative dialogue springs from the need to tell instead of show, this is a more serious problem as it will most likely encompass the rest of the book as well. The solutions are similar to the above, but will be covered in depth in Chapter 11, 'Showing Versus Telling'.

- If informative dialogue comes from your need to control, ask yourself this simple question: Can you let go of wanting to control the scene? Just for an instant, drop your guard. Let the characters overrun you, let *them* take control. It's not going to kill you, and if you don't like the outcome, you can always change it back. Really allow yourself into the character's minds—it is *their* minds you enter. You may have created them, but now you must let them stand on their own. Find out what *they're* about. Find out what they really want to say to each other.

Examples

John saw Mary sitting in the restaurant and walked over to her.

'Hi, Mary,' he said to her. 'I know you come here on Tuesdays and like to sit at this table, which is looking out over the pavement.'

'Yes, John, I do,' she answered. 'And I know you always wear that purple shirt you're wearing with the red dots and white stripes.'

'Yes, Mary, I do,' John said. 'Can I sit down? I know your boyfriend, Henry, whom you've been dating for three years, would not be happy, but I would like to talk to you.'

'Okay, John, sit down,' Mary said. 'But be careful, I know you have a bad leg, which you hurt playing squash, and the doctors had to operate and remove three of your tendons.'

'Yes, I'll be careful. So, I see that you are drinking wine—it is a chardonnay and is white. I see that your glass is three-quarters empty.'

'Yes, it is, John. I see that your hair is parted to the side and that you're wearing a wedding ring on your left hand.'

'Yes, I am, Mary. I see that you're wearing a red dress, which looks nice.'

'Oh, thank you, John. You know already that my mum bought this for me.'

'Yes, I was with you that day.'

'Yes, I remember.'

Here's an example of a writer using dialogue to both convey backstory and describe the setting for the benefit of the reader. But what about the characters? What about their relationship? There is none. It's all fake. They're so preoccupied with conveying information, they never get a chance to *interact* with each other. We see the backstory malady at work when John talks about Mary's boyfriend and Mary talks about John's knee injury. In real life, instead of saying, 'I know your boyfriend, Henry, whom you've been dating for three years, would not be happy,' John would say, 'I know Henry would not be happy.'

He would not *tell* her Henry is her boyfriend or that they've been dating for three years—she *knows* this. Similarly, she wouldn't say, 'I know you have a bad leg, which you hurt playing squash, and the doctors had to operate and remove three of your tendons'; instead she would say, 'I know you have a bad leg.' Forced dialogue like this can often be spotted by looking for key words like 'I know', and 'remember'.

> *'Okay, Dick, what's going on with the Spinoza case?'*
>
> *'I had Charlotte type up all the memos, and we're expecting to close it this week. It'll be an easy win.'*
>
> *'Good, that should mean thousands for our firm.'*
>
> *'Yeah, it should, and that could mean promotions for us.'*
>
> *'But we have to remember that those files are pertinent to our winning the case. Tonight we'll have to go through them one more time and look for any discrepancies. Then, tomorrow, we'll head on up to Austerville and see if we can get any information out of Chuck. Then, after that, we'll go over and see Charlotte and ask her what she thinks about the case.'*
>
> *'That's a good idea. In the meantime, I'll work on getting the information off the computer—you know, the information that will be a big help to us.'*
>
> *'Oh, yes, that's good. You know, if this whole thing goes through, that will mean $300,000 for us in non-negotiable US bonds.'*
>
> *'Yes, I know.'*

Again, note the 'I knows' and 'remembers'. Here, the characters are focused on conveying *future* facts, outlining what's going to happen next, itemizing things that need to be done.

> *'Mr President, here's the situation. Russia has invaded. We just found out. It looks like World War III is here.'*
>
> *'What are our options?'*
>
> *'Well, we have three options. We can launch our missiles, wait to see what happens, or try to make peace.'*

'Launch the missiles,' the president said. 'Here's the key and the code. Let's go down to the war room. Afterward, we'll head to our private bunker underneath the ground, where we go for these kinds of things.'

'Okay Mr President, I'm launching them. Look! Russia is exploding on the map!'

'I see! It's glowing! Look at what we've done. And listen— can't you hear the noise outside?'

'Yes, Mr President. Look, you can see from this window. It is people protesting.'

'They're mad at me. Look, they're shaking the fence. It looks like it might break.'

'Yes. Let's go. The helicopter is here, waiting on the roof.'

This is a most amateur example of dialogue being used to convey events that are actually happening as the characters speak. In these instances, you'll find a lot of imperatives—words like 'look!' and 'watch!' and 'see!' and 'listen!' The juvenility is immediately apparent. We are not watching characters interact in this dialogue, but merely listening to a story unfold—crudely.

Here's a rare example of apparent informative dialogue that *does* work, taken from Franz Kafka's 'In the Penal Colony':

I have been appointed judge in this penal colony. Despite my youth. For I was the former Commandant's assistant in all penal matters and know more about the apparatus than anyone. My guiding principle is this: Guilt is never to be doubted.

On the surface, this may appear to be informative dialogue, but it's not. It seems concerned with conveying the facts of the narrator's job status, but this is a trick: beneath the surface, it's truly concerned with his personality, his voice. The true purpose of this dialogue is to show how insane the speaker is; it mocks him even as it takes him seriously. The information is not put across for its own sake, but for the sake of culminating in his 'guiding principle'.

Let's end with an example from modern literature, from the title story in Steve Lattimore's short-story collection *Circumnavigation*, which illuminates the difference between informative and genuine dialogue:

> *Lockjaw Watkiss is a strapping hillbilly I owe money, sixty bucks or so, from the time he yanked a radiator from one of his rusted junkers—something long and gray and humped—and rigged it to work in my old Datsun. That was about a year ago. Maybe two ....*
>
> *Lockjaw turns to leave, but halfway down the porch steps he notices the Pontiac parked at the side of the house. 'How's that old car of yours running?' he says. 'Toyota, was it?'*
>
> *'Datsun,' I say. 'Not too good. It's at the bottom of a lake.'*
>
> *Lockjaw nods, strokes his long brown beard, stiff as snow. 'That drop-off into the lake behind Jack Stone's Tavern?' he asks.*
>
> *'Yeah.'*
>
> *Lockjaw scratches himself, nods again. 'I know it,' he says. He opens his truck door, lingers for a minute, half in, half out, says, 'There's a helicopter in that lake, you know.'*
>
> *'No kidding.'*
>
> *'Me and the boy used to go look at it sometimes. You can see it when the water's low.'*
>
> *I nod, smile. 'Something,' I say.*

Note how Lattimore sets us up by filling in the backstory of the car; thus, when the time comes, he doesn't need to manipulate the dialogue to convey this information. Instead, he can ascribe genuine dialogue to his characters. He doesn't need to have Lockjaw say, 'Remember, I helped you two years ago, when I gave you that radiator and helped you install it in your car'; instead, Lockjaw can simply ask, 'How's that old car of yours running?'—subtly hinting at the debt the narrator owes him without telling him in the dialogue. And since the dialogue has no fake agenda, the characters have room to speak as they might in real life, free-associating and allowing the conversation to switch direction to the lake.

End-of-Chapter Exercises

- Take a section of dialogue and rewrite it, this time assuming the reader already knows everything he needs to about the story. What would the characters say to each other? Do you feel less pressure to convey information? (You should.) Is your new dialogue different? How so? Can any of these changes be incorporated?
- Take the same section of problematic dialogue, and this time assume the characters already know everything they need to about each other and everything they need to know about what's happened, what's happening, and what will happen. They now have nothing at all they need to say to each other. There is no agenda. What would their new dialogue be like? What are the differences between the new scene and the original? Can any of them be incorporated?
- Now let go of the following three things: (1) the desire to convey any information; (2) the need for any agenda; and (3) the need to control your characters and your plot (as discussed earlier). With this in mind, take two (or more) of your most interesting characters and put them in a room and write a scene between them. How do they interact? How does their relationship blossom? What truths arise? What secret hatreds or jealousies, likes or loves? Now you are learning about your characters, now you are letting *them* teach *you* (whenever you are stumped, you can draw on this exercise). Incorporate any changes that you like.

9

Melodramatic

Who needs children when you have writers?
Anonymous, childless editor

THE second most common type of 'fake' dialogue is melodramatic, or 'Hollywood', dialogue, dialogue that sounds cool, dramatic—but is far from what you'd encounter in real life. Of course, every work has its moments, and the reader does not necessarily want to hear the conversation next door, so dramatic dialogue does have its place, but it must be used seldom, in small doses, and at just the right moment.

The Godfather is a good example. It uses dramatic dialogue throughout—probably more than most films. But if you watch it again, closely, you'll find that the majority of its dialogue is ordinary. Drama is about contrast, and when your manuscript is saturated with drama, it's like crying wolf: the reader won't believe you when the truly dramatic moment comes.

The problem with the homogeneously melodramatic manuscript is that not all characters are melodramatic. (Dostoevsky is an exception. He uses melodrama well and often and it might be argued that virtually all his characters—hysterical, neurotic Russians—are, in truth, melodramatic. But even Dostoevsky's characters are not melodramatic all of the time.) So we are left with yet another instance of the writer imposing his will on the characters and thus another variation on fake dialogue.

The main point is that high drama can be expressed in venues other than dialogue, just as information can be conveyed in other ways. The urge to express drama in dialogue is often a mistake that puts a burden on the dialogue to be the mouthpiece for all the drama in your story. It is inevitable that dialogue of this nature will be forced.

The good news is that melodrama is among the best maladies to have as a writer—it indicates you are striving, putting yourself on the line, going for the dramatic moment. You may either succeed or fail brilliantly—but the effort is worthy either way. True art is about taking chances, and the writer who employs melodrama is on the path of the artist. Furthermore, drama can always be toned down, whereas a manuscript bereft of it cannot necessarily be fixed.

Solutions

- The first step is to identify the melodrama in your dialogue. This can be difficult by yourself, and ideally it is best to call in several objective readers. But there are some ways to at least attempt it yourself, and if you are self-critical enough—especially if you take some time away from your manuscript first—you can develop this skill. Step back and look at several sequences of your dialogue, over the course of one or more chapters. Are they all at the same pitch? Do they brim with the highest possible drama? (Or, conversely, are they ordinary, lacking any drama? Lack of drama can be equally damaging.)
- The second step: determine if within each sequence of dialogue there are identifiable dramatic moments. If so, is there a build-up

to them, a let-down? In other words, is there an arc? Is there contrast?

- Now, looking at several of your sequences of dialogue together, ask yourself: Is there an arc to the sequences as a whole?
- Finally, another way to spot melodramatic dialogue is to look for dramatic turns of events in your plot and examine the surrounding dialogue. Are you compensating for your lack of a dramatic plot twist by stuffing your dialogue with drama? Remember: even the most dramatic moments may have shockingly commonplace dialogue—in fact, this is often preferable, the contrast causing more of a surprise than a dramatic line would. For instance, a boy holding a gun to his head might say to his mother, 'You've ruined my life! You've led me to this! I have nowhere left to turn! I have no other choice!' or he might just say, 'Thanks, Mum' (also see Chapter 15, 'Subtlety').

Examples

'Oh, Henry!'

'Oh, Margaret!'

They ran into each other's arms and embraced for what felt like an eternity.

'Oh, Henry! You know I've loved you so!'

'Oh, Margaret! If only words could express my love for you!'

He picked her up and spun her around in the field of magical, glowing dandelions.

'Oh, darling! What would the world be without you? My love, my sweetness!'

'The world would stop in its tracks without you, my Margarita! I would rather lay my life on the line than miss a moment with you!'

'And I would rather jump off the highest building than miss even one second of the sweet melody of your words!'

They kissed forever as the sun set behind them, a magic golden ball on the horizon, and the birds sang a song just for them.

'Oh, Margaret!'

'Oh, Henry!'

Melodramatic dialogue comes in innumerable forms and the most common is probably romantic. Many writers have a tendency to push love scenes over the edge, to translate strong feelings into strong dialogue. Almost always this is a mistake.

In real life you can usually tell how another person is feeling, regardless of his dialogue. There is something beneath the surface, in his demeanour, his body language—so little, if any of it, is ever expressed in dialogue. The same should hold true on the page. You mustn't think that because it's the written word all feeling, all emotion, all real ways of relating must suddenly be channelled through dialogue. Instead, force yourself to find another way of conveying feeling or emotion.

In the preceding example you'll notice the high drama extends even to the surrounding description—the field of 'glowing dandelions', the 'magic golden ball' of the sun. You'll also notice the abundance of exclamation marks, usually an indicator of melodrama.

Detective Jack Gumshoe sat back in his chair, his feet propped up on the corner of his desk. His hat fell down at an angle, shading his face. The room was dim. A burning cigarette hung from the corner of his mouth.

'Okay, doll,' Detective Gumshoe said. 'Gimme what you got.'

The buxom blonde on the other side of the desk began to talk.

'I want 'em dead, see? Dead as doorknobs.'

'It's gonna cost you.'

'I can pay.'
'But can you afford me?'
'I can afford anybody.'
'How many of 'em?'
'Three. I want it clean.'
'When?'
'Tonight. The cash will be waiting in your mailbox.'
She got up to go.
'And another thing, mister. You never saw me.'
'Just fine by me, lady.'
'Good. And don't get any ideas.'
    Detective Gumshoe inhaled deeply on his cigarette and stubbed it out in the overflowing tray.

Here we have the classic hard-boiled mystery/detective melodrama. Writers in this genre often fall prey to this and must be careful to avoid it—it *sounds* pretty, but in real life no dialogue would come close. More importantly, these characters are not relating to each other; instead, they're merely reciting what the writer thinks are flashy lines. This type of dialogue can often be spotted by short, quick interchanges (like in this example) with few or no pauses in between. In real life, few people think and shoot off smart answers that quickly for that long.

'Oh, Frank! How can you have done it? How can you have cheated on me after all these years!' Jane broke down sobbing. Frank tried to comfort her but she threw his arm away.
    'Jane. What can I tell you? It happens to the best of us. We all get weak sometimes. Life can be difficult. I've lived through so much, Jane.'
    'And the children, Frank! Did you even think of the children? Did you even consider how you were ruining all of our lives?'
    'Jane, you haven't even been here for me for years. You've been like a walking zombie. I haven't felt any love from you, Jane.

Jane, I needed love from you. Why couldn't you give it to me? Why couldn't you give me love, Jane?'

'What will I tell my mother?' Jane sobbed. 'My life is ruined! Ruined!'

'Where am I supposed to go now?' Frank answered, crying himself now. 'How am I supposed to live? All I ever wanted was love!'

'Oh, God help me!' Jane cried. 'I might as well kill myself right now!'

'Oh, God!' Frank cried. 'Why did my life turn out like this? It isn't fair! It isn't fair!'

'Oh!' Jane yelled. 'What's to become of us?'

'It's all over!' Frank cried. 'It's all for nothing!'

The classic domestic melodrama, often found in bad divorce and midlife-crisis movies. After ten lines you feel as if you're suffocating. It can be fun to observe people's private lives as we do in literature, but skilled writers know where to draw the line. Writers of lesser skill, on the other hand, often bring us deeper than we'd like to go—usually by way of melodrama—leaving us with a soiled feeling by the time we've departed. Who wants to know that much about Frank and Jane's personal lives? Who asked for it?

End-of-Chapter Exercises

The following exercises should help you develop skills to express drama in ways other than dialogue.

- Practise conveying drama with silence. Take a scene that you (or an outside reader) may feel is melodramatic and rewrite it completely, this time making use of silence, making the dialogue more quiet. Don't hide from the awkwardness and tension of silence—instead, employ them. For instance, you can have Mary say, 'I love you, John,' and John answer, 'Well, I don't know if I love you, Mary,' or you can simply have John not respond at all. The latter is at least as effective and is more subdued and enigmatic as well.

- Practise understatement. When you complement moments of high drama with words of high drama, you demean the reader. For instance, if A is holding a gun to B's head, and A says, 'You know I really hate you, B! I'm going to kill you!' we know this already by his action of holding the gun. Instead, A should say nothing at all, or if he has to talk, then he should employ understatement, maybe even irony or sarcasm, like, 'I love you, B.' The point is, play against the grain, complementing moments of high drama with subdued dialogue.
- Substitute dramatic character action for dramatic dialogue. Jane could yell and curse at Frank for twenty lines after he tells her he's been cheating on her, or she can turn and take off her wedding ring and flush it down the toilet. It would be just as—if not more—effective. Often, more can be said by one single action than by a character's delivering an entire monologue.

10

Hard to Follow

> ... there's a hormone secreted into the bloodstream of most
> writers that makes them hate their own work while they are
> doing it, or immediately after. This, coupled with the chorus
> of critical reaction from those privileged to take a first look, is
> almost enough to discourage further work entirely.
>
> Francis Ford Coppola, 'Letter to the Reader',
> *Zoetrope* magazine

HARD-TO-FOLLOW dialogue is a malady less commonly
found than those discussed previously, but one that will
almost inevitably lead to the immediate dismissal of a
manuscript. No agent or editor is going to sit there poring over a
manuscript, trying to decipher who is saying what to whom. He
will quickly become frustrated, resenting the writer for not taking
the time to clarify his dialogue.

'Hard to follow' is a deliberately encompassing label because
there are many reasons why dialogue might be hard to follow.
Here are a few of the more often encountered ones:

- The most common is when a writer attempts to capture a certain
  dialect or twang (e.g. Cockney) in dialogue form. He attempts
  to do this in order to make the speech sound more 'genuine',
  or 'real', but often it just ends up impossible to follow, slowing

the reader substantially. This type of dialogue can usually be spotted by an abundance of apostrophes. Similar to this is the heavy use of slang, which can be equally deadly.

- A simpler problem, and one covered in an earlier chapter, is a lack of identifiers (e.g. 'John said', 'Mary said'). It sounds obvious, but many writers string together lines and lines of dialogue without ever stopping to let the reader know who's speaking. This becomes especially complicated when more than two characters are present. A variation on this problem is when a writer uses only 'he said' and we are unsure exactly to whom 'he' is referring.

- Finally, there is the more problematic and rarer 'exclusive' dialogue. This is dialogue that is exclusive of the reader, where interchanges can begin or end in mid-flight, conversation can be exceedingly clipped, and cryptic references abound. Exclusive or cryptic dialogue is rare because it is a form of subtlety, of understatement, and is thus usually the mark of a skilled writer. However, if overused or not used properly—as in much of today's trendy fiction—it can be the mark of self-indulgence.

Solutions

It is nearly impossible for you, as a self-editing writer, to discern whether your dialogue is hard to follow, since, being the one who wrote it, you are obviously able to follow it. However, just going back over your text with an eye for this can help distance you and yield unexpected results.

Some types of confusing dialogue, when found, are more easily fixed than others:

- Dialect, twangs, heavy slang are the most easily fixed—99 per cent of the time just remove them. Even for the most experienced writer, it is often too hard to capture accurately all the nuances of a dialect—and even if it *is* captured perfectly, you'll pay a price: no matter how well done, it will slow down a reader considerably. Is it worth slowing him for something that may or may not pay off? That is up to you—but it had better pay off pretty well.

Another complicating factor is that all readers pronounce words—especially dialect—differently in their heads. Never mind the reader who may have trouble with mispronunciation (as all readers may, to some extent); consider words that can be sounded several ways. For instance, in dialogue, the word 'eh?' might be pronounced 'ā' (long a) or 'ĕ' (short e). Often writers intend certain words to be pronounced a certain way, but they are pronounced differently regardless. Try this simple exercise: take one page from a novel and ask five people (separately) to read it aloud. You'll be amazed by the discrepancies.

Dialect, twangs, and slang can be indicated in other ways, such as preceding description and ancillary character behaviour and temperament. If you are a more experienced writer, you may be able to include *some* dialect or slang, but even then be sparing.

- Problems with identifiers (see Chapter 6, 'Between the Lines') are easy to solve but hard to diagnose for the self-editor (*he* will not have a problem identifying who's speaking). So if you've been told you have a problem in this regard, or think you may, show your manuscript to several competent readers and ask them to go over it specifically with this in mind. Ask where they were confused, how they think the text could be clarified. If your dialogue lacks identifiers, you will probably need to insert some, and if you overuse 'he said', you may need to substitute a character name occasionally.
- Dialogue that is exclusive or cryptic is the hardest to address because a major problem for most writers is cultivating *more*

subtlety. Often, being more cryptic, more clipped, is exactly what is needed.

So, understandably, one is reluctant to dispense the advice particular to this problem: spell things out, let the reader in on what is happening, on what the characters are referring to, stop being so esoteric, so private. This advice must be taken with a grain of salt and only put into practice if you are absolutely sure you suffer from this malady, which is hard to self-diagnose. Verifying it requires the assistance of several good outside readers. It especially requires the assistance of an astute reader—if even *he* has trouble following what's happening, then you can be confident you have a problem.

Examples

'Ya'll wanna know a lit' somthin'?' John asked.

'Wat tat?' Mary asked.

'Tis here roadway's nota gonna be a lettin' tem cars passin' tru here like hellfire.'

'Ain't tat right! Ya'll sat it!'

'Yessir! Tem cars pass tru here like it ain't nobody's damn busine' an' it ain't right at all it ain't!'

'Ain't tat right!'

'An' I know tem cops ain't gonna do wat'ever it'all takes to let 'em wanna head back ter widout knowin' wat they's got in store!'

'Well, whatta ya tink?'

'I ain't know 'cause I ain't gotta see 'em comin'.'

'Look like tem poolice ain't gotta right to ya'll knowin'.'

'Tat wat Joe Bob says.'

'Ain't I know it.'

'Yessir.'

'Well, why ain't ya'll gonna go and tell 'em?'
'I can't be watchin' witout losin' wat I got here.'
'I hear tat.'
'Yessir.'

Here is the effect of poor dialect: the reader's energy is wasted on trying to decipher what they're saying. Dialogue, which should be a respite from the rest of the text, becomes instead a greater burden.

John, Bill, Dave, Sam, Harry, Mary, and Jane sat around the table.
'Would you pass the butter?' he asked.
'To who?' he answered.
'To me,' said a voice.
'Okay, here, would you hand it to him?'
She took it and passed it.
'Why do you always ask me?' she asked.
'Who?'
'You.'
'Do I?'
'Yes. Why don't you ask her?'
'Well, it's not his fault,' another voice said. 'You look like her.'
'Who?'
'You.'
'Me'
'No, her.'
'Well then, why don't you ask her?'
'Will you stop already?' another voice asked.
'Why should I?'
'Because you're making him crazy.'
'Who?'
'Him.'
'He doesn't look crazy. Am I making you crazy?'

'Who?' he asked.
'Me.'
'You?'
'No, her.'
'Yes, you are.'

Here's an example of dialogue that is hard to follow due simply to lack of identifiers—it's impossible to figure out who's speaking! In this extreme case, it's also impossible to figure out both who is the subject of the speech and to whom the speech is being directed. Dialogue this difficult to follow, no matter how well written, will be cause for a manuscript to be put down; no one wants to be put through the agony of having to read a page repeatedly just to figure out who's talking.

John and Dave sat around the living room.
   'Hey,' John said. 'How do you think Linda reacted?'
   'I don't know,' Dave answered.
   'How about Rick?' John asked.
   'He probably thought about Henry,' John answered.
   'Yeah.'
   'Yeah.'
   'So what do you think about Arties?'
   'Not for us.'
   'You think Jewels can hang with them?'
   'Probably.'
   'When do you think they'll reverse this stuff?'
   'Who knows?'
   'I wonder what's happening down at the plant.'
   'They're probably frying Sam.'
   'Yeah, he shouldn't have tied those two together.'
   'Yeah, neither should Bill.'

'Yeah.'
'Yeah.'

What are they talking about? A good example of exclusive dialogue: you feel shut out as a reader, as if you've crashed someone's private party and no one has any intention of filling you in. Notice the plethora of cryptic and personal references, the clipped speech. This type of dialogue is sure to make the reader angry; it seems as if the writer is blatantly disregarding him.

End-of-Chapter Exercises

There are not many exercises you can do to learn to fix confusing dialogue—the main task is to identify where and how it is confusing and clear it up. However, there are one or two things you can work on in general:

• Often, trying to spell out dialect is just an easy way out. Try instead to use some of the actual *vocabulary* (normally spelt) of your subject. This, coupled with mannerisms and tone of voice, will create the desired effect and be much more effective. Study your subject carefully, especially his speech patterns. This time, don't focus on how you might spell out his pronunciations; instead, focus on his *choice* of words, his ways of expression, his body language. For instance, at the end of the film *Sling Blade*, the protagonist, when asked why he is holding a weapon, responds to his adversary, 'I aim to kill you with it.' A lesser writer would have had him say, 'I'm gonna kill you with it,' lazily choosing the cliché 'gonna' in an attempt to capture dialect. This talented writer, with his choice of the unusual 'aim', has utilized dialect in the highest sense—in the choice of words.

- If you get the complaint that your dialogue is exclusive, next time you write, pretend the reader is completely unaware of the subjects being discussed. Make his understanding your number-one concern; make him feel at home, as if he were a guest in your house or a stranger from out of town, even at the risk of telling him something he may already know.

Part III
The Bigger Picture

NINETY-NINE per cent of manuscripts won't even make it to the Bigger Picture, won't even get a chance to be evaluated based upon the criteria laid out in this third section of the book—they will already have been eliminated. If they *do* make it to this section, from an agent's or editor's perspective, this means that *at least* the first five pages will have to be read, and read closely, taking into account not just surface technique, but true content. Indeed, some of the following factors (such as pacing) can take up to fifty pages to evaluate in a good manuscript.

On the other hand, if your manuscript has passed an agent's or editor's preliminary criteria, and he now must consider bigger factors, he may be more agitated: now he *really* has to read. He may scrutinize the following factors with greater vengeance in his rush to get you off his pile. He still is not relaxed and still won't take you seriously. He will do so only (to some extent) after he's got past the first five pages. So you're not there yet. Now is not the time to relax, to let down your guard; on the contrary, now that you've caught his eye, you have an even greater responsibility to deliver, to put your shoulder to the wheel and make sure your manuscript goes that extra mile.

11

Showing Versus Telling

It seems important to me that beginning writers ponder this—
that since 1964, I have never had a book, story or poem
rejected that was not later published. If you know what you are
doing, eventually you will run into an editor who knows what
he/she is doing. It may take years, but never give up. Writing
is a lonely business not just because you have to sit alone in
a room with your machinery for hours and hours every day,
month after month, year after year, but because after all the
blood, sweat, toil and tears you still have to find somebody who
respects what you have written enough to leave it alone and
print it. And, believe me, this remains true, whether the book is
your first novel or your thirty-first.

Joseph Hansen memo, from *Rotten Reviews*

'DON'T tell me you love me. Show me.' What holds
true for real life holds true for the page: a writer can
stop and tell us everything about a character, but
eventually it will become meaningless, just a litany of facts, no
better than a dictionary. It is the writer's job to *show* us what his
characters are like, not by what he says about them, or what they
say about one another, but by their *actions*. A writer can spend a
page telling us his protagonist is a crook, or he can show it in one
sentence, by simply describing his taking a twenty-pound note
from someone's pocket, and letting the reader judge for himself.
The reader will appreciate this latter approach more, because he is

now being given an opportunity to come to his own conclusion about who the protagonist is instead of having the writer tell him what conclusion he should come to. Remember: above all, readers like to make a text their own. This is why they stay with a book: to sympathize, empathize, project. Would you put down your own creation?

The other advantage to showing events instead of telling about them is that it leaves room for a certain amount of ambiguity or interpretation in a text. If a writer tells us his character is a crook, then he is a crook. But if the writer shows the character taking a twenty-pound note, it is up to us to decide if he is a crook. Most of us will assume he is, but some of us may consider other possibilities: perhaps he is taking back money that is already his; perhaps he is helping the person by taking the note because it is counterfeit and was duplicitously planted to entrap him; perhaps there is an ongoing game between the two characters to see who can pick the other's pocket and get away with it, and the money will be returned later. The writer can set up all this with context, but if he does not, if he just shows this isolated incident, there is, indeed, tremendous room for interpretation.

When university students sit around and put forward their interpretations, their way of looking at a text tells us more about *them* than the text; the text becomes a mirror, a blank slate on to which readers project their own state of mind. This is what keeps the best literature endlessly fascinating: twenty students can walk away from a seemingly straightforward text with twenty different conclusions. More interestingly, these same readers may have a different take on the same piece of literature one year later. In that year, they will have read many things, been exposed to new life experiences, and changed as people. Even more so after five years. It can be an entirely different book for them after twenty years away from it. Imagine after fifty: *Moby-Dick* will have two different meanings if read at the age of twenty and then again at seventy. What all this shows is that books are very much about what readers bring to them; no matter how factual the text, there is no absolute reality—it is ultimately subjective. Great books, in order to remain exciting time and again, reflect an awareness of this and leave open this room for interpretation. One of the ways of doing this is avoiding the staid world of laying down facts and, instead, embracing the more expressive, more artistic world of showing.

Another problem with telling is that it makes a text read more like a synopsis than a work of art. With this type of writing, you often walk away feeling as if you've read an outline of a story, a description of what's supposed to happen, of what characters are supposed to be like, but you don't feel as if you've *experienced* any of it, as if you've walked in the characters' shoes, cried or dodged bullets with them. The text will have a 'dry' feeling, and you will never be engaged. True creative writing is an art form like any other art form. Many would argue the main purpose of art is to dramatize, to give people an escape, a venue in which to project, play out, and satisfy their feelings. In order to do this, the reader must enter a world—he cannot have it described to him.

Other art forms, such as music and painting, force the artist to jump right in and create, but writing has a sly ability to allow its practitioners to dodge the artistic. This may be because writing has so many inartistic (or less artistic) manifestations, from legal writing to business writing to official memos to textbooks, where the main priority is not artistic expression but the conveyance of facts. Of course, everything has its place: if it were your responsibility to write down the minutes of your weekly business meetings and as the writer you chose to dramatize these minutes, filling them with emotion, you'd probably get fired.

When you show instead of tell, where you used to have description you will now have a scene. At first glance, this may seem to slow down the text; after all, you had previously conveyed, in less than a page, several major plot events, and now it's taken you ten pages to show just the first of these events. Yes, it does slow things down, especially in terms of number of pages, but it also speeds things up, because the pages that are read will be more enjoyable. Would you rather read ten entertaining pages or one tedious one?

Of course, your book would become weighed down with scenes if you were to show everything, and you'll have to become more selective in deciding which facts you'll convey to begin with. You'll have dramatization where before you had none, and a chief advantage of that is, in the process—if done truly—you will have learned new things about your characters and the turn of events. From your showing will emerge facts that can be useful in future telling.

A book too heavy on showing is also to be avoided—telling has its place. Telling can be particularly useful in establishing narrators and viewpoint characters, and in skilled hands, where the writer is aware of the fact that he is telling but is using it for a purpose. For instance, if a narrator tells us something about another character, what he is really doing is giving us *his* perspective; thus the telling is not really used to tell but to show how the narrator views others. This can be employed with contrast, contradiction. For instance, if the narrator tells us character A is a really nice guy and character A enters the scene and his actions show he is a real idiot, what does this tell us about the narrator's judgement? Or if the narrator tells us he killed character A ten years ago and character A then enters the scene, we might infer our narrator's a liar. Then our not trusting the viewpoint narrator becomes part of the game.

Solutions

- The first step is to spot the areas in your manuscript where you tell when you should show. Likely places are where you use excessive description; where you introduce characters or places for the first time; where there is a flurry of events, a jump in time, or a bridge between major events; where you fill the reader in on backstory; where you (or someone else) generally feel the manuscript to be slow.

  Looked at one way, nearly the whole manuscript can consist of 'problem areas'. You can take almost any piece of information and dramatize it. Deciding what you do and don't want to dramatize is as much an art as the dramatization itself. For now, don't get overzealous. Attack only blatant problem areas.

- Once you've chosen the text you'd like to dramatize, decide how you might go about it. When it comes to dramatization, there are decisions within decisions. Which is the most inherently dramatic fact? Which would make for the best scene? Which would fit best within the scope of the book?

- Replace information with action or events that serve the same purpose. For instance, instead of saying 'his wife was abusive', show her hitting him. Focus on eliminating passages with a dry, synopsis-like feel and replacing them with prose that engages the reader.

- While converting telling to showing, see if there is a way you can leave an element of ambiguity, of mystery, a door open for readers to come to their own conclusions. Take a simple event and consider all the different things it could mean to interpreters—maybe even to yourself. Things happen on many levels in texts, as they do in real life. Some people claim the subconscious mind does not differentiate itself from the

conscious mind; consequently, they suggest, you can interpret baffling real-life events symbolically, the same way you
interpret events in a dream. What might the events in your
text symbolize?

Examples

*The place was heavily barricaded. It was heavily protected. There
was no way any prisoners could get out. It would be impossible to
escape. It was very imposing looking. It was a fortress, a massive
prison. It was very dark inside, too. You couldn't escape on the
ground and you couldn't escape from the roof. It was very far
from any place. The weather was not good.*

One area writers tend to tell instead of show is when describing a
setting. But even with description, there is a way to show instead of
tell. For instance, instead of telling us how heavily fortified the prison
was, the writer could have just stated facts, like 'The walls were made
of stone, twenty feet thick. They were reinforced with bars of tita-
nium, festooning coils of razor wire.' Instead of saying, 'It was very
dark inside,' he could say, 'The guards needed flashlights to patrol
the corridors.' Instead of telling us 'You couldn't escape from the
roof,' he could say, 'Helicopters hovered over the roof, and guards
were stationed every ten feet on parapets, their fingers resting on the
triggers of rifles.' Instead of telling us 'It was far from any place,' he
could say, 'The closest town was a dot on the horizon,' and instead of
saying, 'The weather was not good,' he could say, 'It hadn't stopped
raining in sixteen months,' or any of a number of other things. *Stat-
ing facts is not the same as telling.* 'Telling' directs us to the conclusions we should come to about facts. Facts are just facts.

*He hated her with a vengeance. He told her off. He told her so. He
told her how much he hated her. He told her never to come back*

into his life again. She said words back to him which let him know
that she hated him just as much. The two of them really hated
each other. It was a violent scene. A lot of damage was done. The
neighbours saw everything.

Another common error is summarizing conversations instead of
dramatizing them. For instance, here the writer could just as easily put in quotes 'I hate you, Jane' instead of writing 'He told her
how much he hated her.' Or, more interestingly, he could put in
quotes 'I can't believe I ever liked you,' or he could not put anything in quotes and just say, 'He spat on her.' Instead of writing
'It was a violent scene. A lot of damage was done,' he could say
something like 'She threw a plate at his head. He threw a chair at
her, which missed but went through the window.' Instead of writing 'The neighbours saw everything,' he could say, 'John turned
and caught Mrs Roland peeping through her curtains again, from
across the yard.'

They held up the store. Then they escaped in the car. They were
chased by the police. They eventually outran the police. They spent
the night in a cave. They had sex all night long. They spent the next
day robbing another store. After that, they went to California.
They spent their first three weeks in California robbing more
convenience stores. The second store they robbed, they had a scary
experience. She almost got her ear shot off. They continued rob-
bing stores for another six months. Many crazy things happened.
Then they took a ship to Japan, where they lived for three months.

Can you feel the synopsis-like effect? It is more like an outline of a
story, the result of telling at its extreme. But less egregious errors
still generate the same effect. Virtually any of these sentences can
be developed into a fully-fledged scene (or even many scenes).
The writer here will have to put as much effort into choosing

which of these he wants to dramatize as he does dramatizing them: entire novels have been dramatized with less action.

End-of-Chapter Exercises

- Introduce a new character solely by his actions. Don't tell us a word about him. Let us judge for ourselves. It could be one action, it could be ten.
- Introduce a new character solely by his ambiguous actions. Don't tell us a word about him. Let us judge for ourselves. It could be one action, it could be ten. Ask three readers to tell you what they think of him. If their conclusions are different, that's good.
- Introduce a new location solely by describing it. Don't tell us what it's like. Just describe it. Let us come to our own conclusions. Is it scary? Imposing? Barren? Evoke the mood by the description, not by telling us what the mood is.
- Practise manipulating telling for your own ends. Don't use it in the traditional sense; instead, use it as a character-viewpoint trick. Have character A tell us about character B, not for us to learn about character B, but to learn character A's perspective. Is character A prejudiced? Is he a liar? Does he come to premature judgements? Try to convey each of these and you'll begin to see that 'telling' can be used for not telling at all.

12

Viewpoint and Narration

Stephen King's first four novels were rejected. 'This guy from Maine sent in this novel over the transom,' said Bill Thompson, his former editor at Doubleday. Mr Thompson, sensing something there, asked to see subsequent novels, but still rejected the next three. However, King withstood the rejection, and Mr Thompson finally bought the fifth novel, despite his colleagues' lack of enthusiasm, for $2,500. It was called *Carrie*.

WHAT distinguishes fiction from other forms of writing is that before you can set down a word you must first decide: (1) from whose viewpoint you will tell the story; and (2) whether you will use a first-, second-, or third-person narrator. Mastery of viewpoint and narration requires a fair amount of technical skill, thus it is not surprising many amateur writers are revealed in this way. Viewpoint and narration comprise a delicate, elaborate facade, in which one tiny break or inconsistency can be disastrous, the equivalent of striking a dissonant chord in the midst of a harmonious musical performance.

There are many ways viewpoint and narration can be problematic. Here are some of the more common ones:

• The most obvious problem is inconsistency among forms of narration, for instance when a writer switches from first ('I') to second ('you') to third ('he' or 'she') person, or from singular

('I') to plural ('we'). Once you choose a form of narration, you should stick to it; switching will disorient a reader. This is such a fundamental mistake, it is rarely encountered, but when it is, it is cause for instant rejection.

- Related to this are inconsistencies or frequent switches between viewpoint characters. The method of narration (for example, first person) might be consistent, but the viewpoint behind it might switch. Suddenly, the 'I' that was originally our protagonist, Henry, becomes a different 'I', say a man named John. What happened? We become confused as readers.

  There are books that employ multiple viewpoints to great advantage—indeed, where multiple viewpoints are integral to the story—such as Terry McMillan's *Waiting to Exhale* or Kent Meyers' *The River Warren*. However, when writers such as these employ viewpoint switches, they never switch in mid-sentence, mid-paragraph, or mid-chapter, as some amateur writers do. Instead, they only switch viewpoints in conjunction with a clear break, such as a line, chapter, or book break. This makes it less disorienting for the reader. Additionally, the switches are truly integral to their story (as in, say, a murder mystery where five different characters witness a murder and each sees something different, and a chapter from each perspective complements the story). Many amateur writers, on the other hand, switch viewpoints solely because they like the idea, because they think it adds spice. In general, I would strongly recommend beginning writers not to employ multiple viewpoints; developing one good viewpoint character can be hard enough, even for the most experienced writer.

- Another common problem is when viewpoint characters know information they cannot. For instance, if we are being told a story from the first-person viewpoint of a killer, he cannot tell us what his victims are thinking. One of the advantages of a limited viewpoint is that we get inside the character's head; but the disadvantage is that, by definition, we cannot then enter anyone else's head.

• A common problem is a viewpoint character with no real viewpoint, no voice, no originality. It's as if he's not even there. While in the long run this can be serious, in the short run—the first five pages—this type of problem can be difficult to spot. In other words, in running down our list, this may not be an added plus, but it's not going to seriously hurt you initially. If all else is well, you'll probably be able to sneak by without a real, distinctive viewpoint, but at the end of the day it *will* hurt. (While a viewpointless narrator leads to an unengaging manuscript, conversely, an overly engaging viewpoint can suffocate a text—and this can be detected quickly.)

The reader must feel strongly about the narrator. It is just as good to dislike as to like him—the only error is to have the reader not care either way. At one point in the film *Private Parts,* one radio executive says to another that the majority of the people who make up Howard Stern's ratings are people who *dislike* him. They tune in for the same reason his fans do: they want to hear what he's going to say next. Whether they like or dislike him doesn't matter—what matters is that they are compelled, that they don't want to tune out. Even for the ardent feminist, it would be more compelling to read a book from the perspective of a womanizer, bragging about his exploits, than it would to read about someone detailing his filing duties. The feminist reader might hate the womanizing narrator with a passion, but she probably won't put the book down. Love and hate are two sides of the same coin anyway—it's evoking the emotions, getting the reader to care at all, that is the real feat.

Solutions

The main point of these solutions is for you to question your existing technique—and perhaps replace it—as opposed to just plunging ahead with whatever viewpoint and narration initially propelled the text, or whatever 'sounded right', which is what most writers tend to do.

- If you're going to tell the story through one character's viewpoint, the first thing to do is take a step back and ask yourself which character can offer the most compelling perspective. Who is the most (or least) interesting, the most (or least) opinionated? Who could flavour the text? As I said before, I don't suggest, at least to start, that you tell the story through the viewpoints of many characters. Unless handled expertly, this often ends up creating a detached, synopsis-like feeling in a text, as it becomes hard to get involved with any one character.
- Once you've chosen your viewpoint character, look at your narration. First-person narration ('I') is distinctive and intimate, but it can also be limiting and overly stylistic. It draws magnified attention to the prose, so I would not recommend it for the beginning writer, as it can often put your story in the background and writing in the foreground. Second-person narration ('you') is rarely encountered; it is extremely stylistic and nearly impossible to keep up for more than a page or two. Third person ('he' or 'she') is most frequently used because it can be both intimate and detached at the same time.
- Now on to specific problems. If you have inconsistencies or breaks in narration (e.g. you switch from first person to third), take them out and stay with only one form of narration, for the reasons mentioned above.
- If you employ switches in viewpoint within the same sentence, paragraph, or chapter, rewrite so that you stay with only one viewpoint at least until you reach a line break (preferably a chapter break). In most manuscripts, viewpoint should not be switched at all, but if you feel compelled to switch, at least do it in a place that will make it less disorienting for the reader. What

most writers don't understand is that, if they feel compelled to switch, often the reason behind the compulsion is that the original viewpoint character is not that interesting to begin with. So, before you switch, (1) ask yourself if these switches are truly integral to the story, and (2) first try to develop your original viewpoint character (or find a new one) so that he is so compelling you feel no need to switch.

- If you have viewpoint characters who know things they can't, take this out. John should never know what Mary is thinking (unless he is psychic, which would have to be part of his character). You can get around this, though, by having John *guess* (internally or aloud) what Mary's thinking. This is more interesting anyway, as it leaves room for ambiguity and expectation.

Examples

I was walking down the street when I ran into Mary. She looked fine. He thought she looked better than last time. He wished he had said hello to her. We went together to the shop and the whole time we were complaining. I wondered if I would ever see her again. He kept dwelling on the fact and we couldn't get any rest. You think this is strange, don't you? You think we're crazy. You wonder.

Here is what switch in narration does for you: see how confusing it is? Notice the switch from first person to third person in line 1, to first person plural in line 3. After a few more switches, we finally have a switch, in line 6, to second person. Who is 'he' referring to in line 2? Is this the same 'he' as the first person narrator? Who are the 'we' in line 3?

John saw Mary, and he thought she looked fine. He was nervous as he went up to her and asked her to dance. He kept rehearsing the words in his head. He finally reached her after what seemed like an eternity to him. He felt himself sweating, fidgeting with his hands. He wondered suddenly if he looked all right. He tapped her on the shoulder and smiled the best he could as she turned around. Mary looked back at him and smiled. She thought he looked cute.

Which is the offending line? If you said the last one, you are correct. As you can see, this entire paragraph is from John's perspective; we are clearly in his shoes. So for the writer to suddenly tell us that Mary 'thought he looked cute' is unacceptable. It is jarring, inconsistent with the intention of the paragraph. It is a classic example of a poorly timed switch in viewpoint. One could argue that, if this is an omnisciently narrated manuscript, there is room for Mary's perspective. Perhaps, but even then it wouldn't come at the end of John's paragraph; it would, rather, initiate a new paragraph.

I watched all the children playing in the park and wondered if Mary would ever want to have kids. It had been ten years and she kept saying she would, but time was running short. Who knew if she'd ever give in? The sun was beating down and it was getting too hot on the bench. I looked at my watch and realized it was time to go. I looked over at the kids one last time. They were playing on the slides. They were thinking of their mothers and of what they would eat for dinner. They were getting tired.

Again, the final two sentences are the offending ones. The 'I' narrator could not possibly know what these children are thinking or how they are feeling. Something like this could be fixed easily by simply prefacing it with '*I could tell* they were thinking of their mothers.' This way it is conjecture, not fact, and we thus never leave our viewpoint character's perspective.

Let's look at viewpoint in the hands of a master. Here's the opening paragraph of Flannery O'Connor's classic short story 'Everything That Rises Must Converge':

Her doctor had told Julian's mother that she must lose twenty pounds on account of her blood pressure, so on Wednesday nights Julian had to take her downtown on the bus for a reducing class at the Y. The reducing class was designed for working girls over fifty, who weighed 165 to 200 pounds. His mother was one of the slimmer ones, but she said ladies did not tell their age or weight. She would not ride the buses by herself at night since they had been integrated, and because the reducing class was one of her few pleasures, necessary for her health, and free, she said Julian could at least put himself out to take her, considering all she did for him. Julian did not like to consider all she did for him, but every Wednesday night he braced himself and took her.

At first glance, this seems as if it's from the viewpoint of Julian's mother; but if you look closely, it is actually Julian's viewpoint. First, 'she' is never named but only referred to as 'Julian's mother'; second, if you noticed the last sentence, it begins with 'Julian did not like'. When a writer tells us what a character likes, he puts us in his viewpoint. At no point in this paragraph does it say outright what Julian's mother likes or thinks, only what she says, all of which, we realize in the end, is funnelled through Julian's lens. This is a rare example indeed, as the protagonist's viewpoint is not firmly established until the last line; O'Connor exhibits masterful endurance in allowing the ambiguity of viewpoint, but also knows we can't get past the first paragraph without being implanted in *some* viewpoint. She has also, in the same short space, introduced two characters, delineated their relationship, filled us in on the backstory, let us know what her characters' future holds in store, and given us a firm sense of direction. All in one paragraph, and none at the expense of the other.

End-of-Chapter Exercises

• Viewpoint and narration are so subjective, with so many possible manifestations, the most helpful thing to do is expose yourself to as many different approaches as possible. Go back and reread some of the classics with only this in mind, studying authors' approaches to viewpoint and narration. Instead of just appreciating their texts as a reader, you will begin to appreciate them as a *writer*. You will begin to understand why these writers made many of the choices they did. Also observe how viewpoint and narration, when handled well, can add so much to a text. Look at Camus's *The Stranger* and Dostoevsky's *Notes from Underground*, two books driven by equally powerful narrators who nonetheless could not have more different approaches—and yet who both are responsible for making their texts what they are.

• Take a scene from your manuscript and rewrite it in at least three different ways, each influenced by a different facet of your narrator's character. What changes come about? Did his viewpoint, when coming to the fore, actually modify events? (In most cases, it will.) Which of these changes can be incorporated? Now you will have a text that arises from the character, instead of one imposed on him.

• Take a scene and change the method of narration. If you are using first person, switch to third and vice versa. Any differences? How does it change the character? The text? Can you incorporate any of these changes?

13

Characterization

Bill Thompson, the same editor who discovered Stephen King, years later bought a first novel from a man named John Grisham. It was called *A Time to Kill*. Thompson paid $15,000 for it, on behalf of Wynwood Press. It didn't earn back its advance.

Grisham and his agent came back to Thompson with a new manuscript (titled *The Firm*), already optioned by Tom Cruise. They knew they could get big money for it elsewhere, but Grisham, out of loyalty to Thompson, offered it to him for only $50,000. Thompson wanted to take him up on the offer, but the management of Wynwood was less keen. After all, 'optioned' didn't mean 'made', and Grisham still hadn't made back the money on his first book, and even if he had, the management of a smaller publisher like Wynwood didn't want to risk that kind of money on a novel. So Grisham and his agent went elsewhere. Another publisher ended up buying *The Firm* with a bid well into six figures.

The Firm was a *New York Times* number one bestseller, as has been every Grisham novel since.

To say one can determine a writer's proficiency at characterization within the first five pages is a bold statement and sometimes untrue. However, it can be true in some instances, particularly when characterization is misused, which can lead to the dismissal of a manuscript, sometimes within one page.

The poor usage of character names, for instance, may signal an amateur on a surface read. There are many ways one might bungle this:

- Switching between first and last names. For instance, referring to a character as 'John Smith' in the first sentence, then 'Mr Smith' in the second, then 'John' in the third, then 'Smith' in the fourth, and so on. It is hard enough for a reader to learn a new character—don't make it harder by being inconsistent in the way you refer to him. This can become especially confusing when there are many characters in the scene. If John Smith is being called five different names and there are three other characters in the room, also being called by different names, that makes for twenty names the reader will have to commit to memory, instead of just four. Think about it: when you are introduced to half a dozen people at a party, it is not easy to commit all their names to memory—the reader's predicament is no different when reading your manuscript.
- The use of stock, clichéd, or overly exotic names. A manuscript filled with 'John Smiths' and 'Mary Does' will more often than not be indicative of a stock or cliché mentality. This will end up being reflected in the rest of the writing, or at least in the characters themselves. Conversely, a manuscript filled with people named 'Zooba' and 'Raylazan' indicates a writer striving too hard to be different (usually as overcompensation for not having a more original story). Names like these are also hard for a reader to remember and can easily become annoying.

Moving on to characterization itself, there are a number of fairly common problems that can be detected in the opening pages. These include:

- Launching into the story without stopping to establish any of the characters. This is found in many 'high concept' novels, which often open with a heated scene, the plot unfolding immediately. But in the midst of all the excitement these writers seem to forget we haven't even met their characters, who often turn out to be no more than props.

- The presence of stock or clichéd characters and/or character traits. We've all seen novels peopled by characters like the Russian spy, the mad scientist, the hardened private detective. In most cases, these characters end up being as unoriginal as we might expect. Clichéd character *traits*, however, can plague even the most advanced novelist. Every writer slips now and again, and sometimes even superbly original characters exhibit stock traits or actions.

- The introduction of too many characters at once. No reader can possibly keep in his head all twelve astronauts introduced on page 1, all ten conspirators around the table, all eight friends chatting in the living room. It will have the opposite effect: instead of remembering many characters, we'll remember none.

- Confusion over who the protagonist is. Some novels end up being equally dominated by several characters; they keep progressing, and we're still not sure whose story it is, who we should care about. This is most commonly found with the use of multiple viewpoints. (See Chapter 12, 'Viewpoint and Narration' for a more in-depth discussion.)

- The presence of extraneous characters. It takes a great deal of effort to make mental room for a new character. Don't waste a reader's energy by introducing a character who ends up making just one appearance if he has no greater significance or does not further the plot. You can get away with this to some extent in a screenplay, where it is a more common device, but beware of

thinking like a screenwriter when it comes to a novel, infusing
your text with these walk-on roles.

- Generic character description. There is nothing terribly wrong
  with generic character description, but there is nothing right
  about it, either. We're all tired of being introduced to the man
  in his forties, of medium height and weight, with brown hair
  and brown eyes. This sort of thing may not necessarily hurt
  you, but on the other hand, if the description is unique, it
  may help.

- Characters we don't care about. One of the hardest things to
  do in writing is to create characters that readers will care about,
  that will make them *have* to read on. Often I read a novel that
  is good, with characters that are solid, but I just don't care that
  much about them. I don't dislike them, but I'm not necessarily
  compelled by them (or their situation), either.

- The unsympathetic protagonist. Occasionally one encounters
  a protagonist so entirely unsympathetic—like the bully or wife
  beater or child molester—as to make you want to put the book
  down immediately. Protagonists can be compelling—even
  likeable—without being upstanding human beings. We love,
  for instance, Dr Lecter in *The Silence of the Lambs*, even though
  he is a murdering cannibal. But if you're going to create such
  a character, you must devote a great deal of time and space to
  making him likeable. It is not something I would recommend
  for the beginner—creating likeable characters is hard enough
  without starting off with a murderous personality.

Solutions

Character problems can be easy—or virtually impossible—to fix,
depending on the type of problem and its severity. Let's look at a
few of the more common ones.

- Character names are, of course, the most easily fixed. If you refer to a character in several different ways (e.g. first, then last name), just stop doing it. Choose one way of referring to him and stick to it. You may think you're adding 'variety' by referring to the same person in all these different ways, but you're not. What you're doing is pulling the reader's attention to the writing itself and thus away from the action. Remember: every time you refer to a character in a different way, it is the equivalent of the reader's having to learn an entirely new name.

- If you've used stock character names, rack your brain and come up with something new. Do some research. There are books of names. You can look to mythology, the Bible. In ancient times, no one was named haphazardly—every name had some deeper significance. It is only in modern times that we have strayed from this, arbitrarily naming children whatever sounds nice. Consider the character's ethnicity, locale, religion, and social class. For instance, a boy in a religious Jewish family would never be a Matthew or Christopher, just as a boy from a religious Catholic background would not be a Moses or Abraham. You don't want to use blatant symbolism—e.g. naming your character 'Zeus' or 'Eve'—but you don't want to skim over a name's significance, either.

    If, on the other hand, you've employed names that are too exotic, remember: the originality of your manuscript should show in the *characters*, not their names. Even if you are creating a completely alien world—as in a science-fiction novel—this doesn't necessarily mean the names must also be foreign. In fact, it would be even stranger to find a 'Bob' in another galaxy!

- If you've launched into your story without stopping to establish characters, remember: story is as much (if not more) about characters as about plot. *They* are your plot—their needs, wishes, developments. Their introduction and establishment should be foremost in your mind. Even if you begin with heavy plot action, character introduction should be integral to this action. And the action of the plot should not be just for its own sake, but should also serve to further the growth of the participating characters.

- If you've peopled your novel with unoriginal characters, created only as instruments to serve the plot, then it's time to think again. We all instinctively are inclined to put down on paper what we've seen and heard before—especially when we're rushing to set down a story—but you must fight against this. One way of doing so is to have your stock character do the opposite of what's expected of him. For instance, instead of the cynical private detective, how about the *happy* or *naive* private detective who doesn't smoke, doesn't drink, who can't stop smiling? This certainly would take a stereotype and turn it on its head. The beauty of an original character is that your plot will often grow out of him, instead of vice versa. For instance, having created our happy, naive detective, can't you imagine a hundred stories revolving around him? Maybe it's his first case, maybe it's a comedy, maybe it's an otherwise serious story with this bizarre twist.

  As far as clichéd traits are concerned, we all fall into this trap. Creating a unique character is only the first step—it takes ongoing work to keep him original. All is not lost if some of his traits or actions are unoriginal; you can still keep him, just change those traits.

- If you have a tendency to introduce many characters at once, learn patience. Figure out ways of staggering them (one obvious way is having them enter the room not together but, say, ten minutes apart). See if you can possibly hold off introducing some characters until later in the book (you can create a plot element to allow for this). If you must introduce them all at once (for instance, if they are in a gang, or need to be associated together), then don't spend your first ten pages chronicling all of them. Focus on some, ignore others for now. You can switch the focus later.

- Remember: it is hard for a reader to enter a new world, harder still if he is unsure who your protagonist is. Think of when you moved into a new neighbourhood. Suddenly, everything's different, you don't know anybody. So make it easy on him. Right away, give him a friend, a guide, someone to follow. Once he is firmly in the world, once he is oriented, *then* let him look around. But first make sure he is hooked, or else risk losing him. If you're using an omniscient viewpoint, try using first or third person instead (see Chapter 12, 'Viewpoint and Narration').

- If you've included extraneous characters, remove them. You might spend too much time describing a waiter, for instance, or perhaps you have a minor character who makes many appearances but doesn't further the plot. In the more advanced levels (beyond the scope of this book), there are other things to look for, such as characters being extraneous because their function mirrors that of others, detracts from others, or doesn't provide enough contrast. As a rule of thumb, keep your number of characters to an essential minimum and never introduce anyone by name unless they're significant.

- If your character description is generic, there are many possible solutions. First, it's easier for the reader to remember an unusual-looking character; for instance, a man with a missing leg. If there is nothing striking about him, it is your job to describe him in a way that makes him striking. If you are perceptive enough, you can find something unusual about almost anyone, even the most commonplace looking character. As with naming your character, consider ethnicity, locale, religion, and social class when describing him. If there's nothing striking about his appearance, think of his demeanour, his inner or emotional life. For instance, you might say, 'He looked as if he'd been through one too many divorces.'

Character description is difficult because it inevitably stops the action and is ultimately a form of telling instead of showing. But it is the writer's job to work around this, to convey description without stopping the flow. The most experienced writers can do this. Many amateur writers, however, bring their manuscripts to a halt to describe their characters with obvious ploys such as 'John was walking down the hall. He stopped and looked in the mirror. He looked at his brown eyes, his brown hair ...'. Try not to convey description in such a contrived, ordinary way.

Additionally, try to utilize a less expected vocabulary for character description (see Chapter 4, 'Comparison', where we discuss vocabulary). For instance, instead of 'brown' eyes, you might call them 'almond'; instead of saying 'He was a large, healthy man', you might call him 'ursine'. Use comparison. Instead of saying 'His eyes were blue', you could say 'His eyes were the colour of the tiles beneath his feet.' Finally, don't describe just the usual characteristics, such as eyes, lips, nose, hair. Describe *around* them. For instance, in addition to describing the colour of his eyes (which everyone does) you can describe other things about them, such as 'His eyes were sunken in his head. They were set close together and abnormally large, giving him the appearance of a ghoul.' Or, instead of saying 'His hair was blond', you might say, 'His pale hair was set too far back on his head, prematurely receded for a man his age. There was a blatant bald spot, and unhealthy strands hung from the sides.'

Following are four examples from classic literature where we see how character description, when handled expertly, can benefit a book. Here we have a description of Marlow in Joseph Conrad's *Heart of Darkness*:

He had sunken cheeks, a yellow complexion, a straight back, an ascetic aspect, and with his arms dropped, the palms of hands outwards, resembled an idol.

Note the traits Conrad has chosen to describe: 'cheeks', 'complexion', posture, 'aspect'. These are unusual choices, and the adjectives he uses are equally unusual: 'sunken' cheeks; 'yellow' complexion; 'straight' back; 'ascetic' aspect. He doesn't stop there—as many writers would—but goes further and tells us the overall impression these traits make: Marlow's resemblance to an 'idol'.

He had not been listening very attentively, the glare of the sun in the shadeless valley was altogether too strong, it was difficult to collect one's thoughts. All the more did he admire the officer, who in spite of his tight-fitting full-dress uniform coat, amply befrogged and weighed down by epaulettes, was pursuing his subject with such enthusiasm and, besides talking, was still tightening a screw here and there with a spanner.

A masterful example (from Kafka's 'In the Penal Colony') of a character being described without interfering with the action. In the midst of telling us what the character is doing— 'tightening a screw here and there'—Kafka describes him, almost as an aside. This is deliberate. He has also chosen to describe aspects of the character that complement the action. For instance, in the midst of establishing the setting—in this case the climate—he has chosen to describe the character's dress (which incidentally tells us volumes). If Kafka had chosen instead to describe the character's facial features, it would have conflicted with the action. Note also how, like Conrad, Kafka does not describe the character for the sake of description, but for the sake of making a greater impression: in this case, that the narrator 'admired' him for his dress. This is another powerful tool to use when describing a character: instead of simply describing a character, also tell us how your viewpoint character *reacts* to his description. (For instance, instead of writing 'She had red hair', you might write, 'He hated her red hair, which was too short and brought back memories of his grandmother.') In Kafka's case, the narrator 'admired' the officer, and this makes an impression on us as readers, suggests that we, too, might admire him; it also tells us something about our narrator, as we learn what his values are, what he admires in people. Also note his unusual usage of vocabulary, words such as 'befrogged' and 'epaulettes'.

He was an inch, perhaps two, under six feet, powerfully built, and he advanced straight at you with a slight stoop of the shoulders, head forward, and a fixed from-under stare which made you think of a charging bull. His voice was deep, loud, and his manner displayed a kind of dogged self-assertion which had nothing aggressive in it. It seemed a necessity, and it was directed apparently as much at himself as at anybody else. He was spotlessly neat, apparelled in immaculate white from shoes to hat, and in the various Eastern ports where he got his living as ship-chandler's water-clerk he was very popular.

Here we have the opening of Conrad's *Lord Jim*. Note how, instead of saying, 'He was five feet ten', Conrad says, 'He was an inch, perhaps two, under six feet', which seems to serve the same purpose, but is actually quite different. It gives the narration some style, some flourish, which works here since it is the opening line (see Chapter 14, 'Hooks'); more importantly, it connotes that no one knows for sure how tall he is, which is significant given that conflicting accounts of this character are integral to the story. Note how Conrad says he 'advanced' at you, mentions the 'stoop' of his shoulders, the angle of his head, his type of 'stare'; these are traits most writers would never consider. Additionally, Conrad takes all these traits and again forms an impression, that of a 'charging bull', in this case also employing simile. 'His manner displayed a kind of dogged self-assertion' is another unusual choice, but to finish the sentence with 'which had nothing aggressive in it' is masterful. It is a breaking of stereotype. 'It seemed a necessity, and it was directed apparently as much at himself as at anybody else' is taking the impression of this character's traits to the most profound level—and this all within the opening few sentences. Already, we not only know what he looks like, but we know him. Conrad goes on to describe him as 'spotlessly neat', another unusual choice. Colour—of clothes, skin, eyes, hair—can be a distinguishing factor and is here: 'apparelled in immaculate white from shoes to hat'. Finally, Conrad concludes with his being 'popular', a way of telling us how others react to him, just as Kafka did with his narrator who 'admired' the officer.

He was obeyed, yet he inspired neither love nor fear, nor even respect. He inspired uneasiness. That was it! Uneasiness. Not a definite mistrust—just uneasiness—nothing more. You have no idea how effective such a ... a ... faculty can be. He had no genius for organizing, for initiative, or for order even. That was evident in such things as the deplorable state of the station. He had no learning, and no intelligence. His position had come to him—why? Perhaps because he was never ill.... He had served three terms of three years out there.... Because triumphant health in the general rout of constitutions is a kind of power in itself.... Once when various tropical diseases had laid low almost every 'agent' in the station, he was heard to say, 'Men who come out here should have no entrails.' He sealed the utterance with that smile of his, as though it had been a door opening into a darkness he had in his keeping.

Our final example comes from Conrad's *Heart of Darkness*. Conrad is not concerned with surface description, but with getting to the deepest core of this character. He has chosen to focus on aspects of his personality relevant to the setting, thus again we have description that complements the action. Note how Conrad opens with 'He was obeyed', another example of describing a character by the way others react to him. He then uses his character's traits as a way of commenting on humankind in general, not stopping with 'he inspired uneasiness', but continuing with 'You have no idea how effective such a ... faculty can be'. He does not stop with 'His position had come to him—why? Perhaps because he was never ill', but goes on to say, 'Because triumphant health in the general rout of constitutions is a kind of power in itself.' Here we have character description being used to its full potential, not just to describe one man, but to penetrate the deepest truths of Man as a whole. To summarize the character, Conrad concludes with a quotation of his: 'Men who come out here should have no entrails,' an enigmatic and vaguely sinister utterance, one that perfectly encapsulates him as a man who places more value on work than on life, and ultimately offers a subtle hint at his view of the entire policy of colonization.

- Characters we simply don't care about are the hardest to fix. If a character that you want to be sympathetic has a certain trait that makes him unsympathetic (such as hitting his wife), this can be fixed easily enough: simply take it out. But if a character is just generally unalluring, how you might make him alluring is entirely subjective. It is easy for a reader to describe something specific he doesn't like about a character, but nearly impossible for him to say why a character is not compelling to him. He just doesn't care about him. This is a problem that extends beyond the scope of this book; this writer needs to do long-term work on character development and is best referred to an in-depth study of characterization (there are many books on this alone). One word of advice may be helpful: what's interesting to you may not be to someone else. Be less solipsistic; consider what makes a character intriguing to others. Readers don't want the ordinary, the everyday; they want to be captivated. Ask yourself: Are your characters interesting, or are they engrossing?

Examples

Bill Davis entered the cockpit. There were twenty people there waiting to greet him. First, there was Jack, the commander. He was tall and broad. Next to Jack was Harry, the second in command. He was thin and short. Behind Harry was Paul, a bright, cheery man. Next to Paul was Dave, an old friend of Bill's from school. On the other side were Rudy, Charlie, Sam, and Tom. Rudy was old. Charlie was young. Sam was fat. Tom was skinny. Beside them were Steve ....

Here we have an inundation of characters. Who can possibly compartmentalize all these people at once? Either these characters would have to be introduced over a long period of time, or the entire set-up would need to be rethought, with some of them removed.

Private Detective Jack Smith sat behind his desk. He reached into his shirt pocket and brought out his Zippo lighter. He lit up his cigarette and dragged hard on it. He took a swig from his flask.

He had been trying to quit both but gave it up. He was tired of the whole damn business and promised himself no more cases. He had been having a long affair with his secretary. He didn't want to deal with the wife. Bills were always too high. He wanted to get out, but just couldn't give up the fast life.

Here we have a fairly stock character: the worn out private eye. Who wants to read about another PI? Stock characters come in many forms. Always be on guard, and even if your character isn't stock, be careful not to allow him stock characteristics as you proceed.

John and Mary sat in their favourite restaurant. This was an important night in their lives. John was about to propose to Mary. He had bought her this great big ring with all his money. She must have sensed it; she seemed happy already. They ate dinner and danced all night. The waiter came along and asked them what they'd like for dessert. The waiter's name was Fred. He'd been working there for three years. John and Mary said, 'Nothing, thanks.' Later, John proposed. Mary was so happy. She said yes.

Who cares about the waiter? Who cares that his name is Fred, that he'd been working there for three years? A classic example of an extraneous character. You'll notice that he not only takes up space but also interrupts the action at a pivotal moment.

End-of-Chapter Exercises

Characterization is a long, arduous, and ever-developing process. Don't be discouraged. The longer you consciously work at it, the better you'll become.

• Reread great works of literature, carefully observing how various writers handle characterization and character description.

- Pay close attention to those around you in your daily life—at work, at home, on the street—and consciously record any interesting or unusual traits or habits that you can use for your characters (even if at first you can't find any, the very act of observation will make you more astute).

- Take one of your characters whom you fear is stock and turn him around—make him do the exact opposite of what might be expected from a character like him. This alone could help spark interesting scenarios. For instance, a teacher who won't teach (or who teaches misinformation), a fireman who starts fires (*Fahrenheit 451*), a policeman who steals (*The Bad Lieutenant*), a teenage gang leader who likes classical music. Go against the grain.

14

Hooks

INTERVIEWER: The literary world seems so much more vicious than the music or art worlds. There's a lot more nastiness.

MARTIN AMIS: I'll tell you why. When you review a piece of music, you don't sing a song about it; when you review an art exhibition, you don't paint a painting about it. But when you review prose fiction, you write prose fiction about it. And don't tell me that particular journalist is satisfied, or never had ambitions to become more than a journalist.

From 'Conversations', *Icon* magazine, June 1998

SOME first lines are so powerful that you absolutely have to keep on reading. This is known as a 'hook'. Nearly all the great writers employ hooks in one form or another, from Melville's 'Call me Ishmael' (*Moby-Dick*) to Camus's 'Maman died today. Or yesterday maybe, I don't know' (*The Stranger*) to Kafka's 'As Gregor Samsa awoke one morning from uneasy dreams, he found himself transformed in his bed into a gigantic insect' ('The Metamorphosis').

Despite popular misconception, though, the hook is more than a marketing tool. At its best, it can be not only a propellant but also a statement of what you might expect from the text to come. It can establish a character, narrator, or setting, convey a shocking piece of information. The irony is that there is only so much you can do with one line; thus, it is a game: the less space you have to work with, the more creative you must become. It is not surprising then that hooks comprise some of the most memorable lines in literature.

What is rarely discussed is the importance of the hook not only as an opening line but as an opening *paragraph*, not only as an opening paragraph but as an opening *page*, not only as an opening page but as an opening *chapter*. In other words, the same intensity of thought applied to the opening line should not be confined to the opening line—a common malady—but rather applied to the text in its entirety. This takes endurance, focus, and concentration; with this level of intensity, it may take several days to complete even one paragraph.

Look at your first or last line and think of the agonizing effort you put into it. You knew you were in the spotlight, that it had to be good. How many times did you rewrite that one line? What would the rest of your manuscript be like if you agonized over each line in the same way? *It would take forever* is probably your first thought. Now you're thinking. Wagner spent thirty-six years on *Parsifal.* Margaret Mitchell spent a decade researching and writing *Gone with the Wind.* Ovid, the Roman poet, said one should wait nine years after finishing one's work before seeking publication. Here lies the difference between someone writing for money and a *writer*.

Thus we come to another distinction between an average writer and a great one: Does the intensity of the hook end with one line? One paragraph? One page? Of course, an opening line is a special thing, and it is nearly impossible to maintain its intensity for an entire text—yet we can look to see if there is at least some sustenance, if some traces remain. I am often amazed by how many manuscripts begin with good first lines—and good openings in general—and then fall apart; it is actually rare to see the intensity found in a first (or last) line maintained throughout a manuscript.

To get a good idea of a hook that extends past a first line, let's look at the opening of Dostoevsky's *Notes from Underground*—a hook that both extends to an entire paragraph and establishes the narrative voice:

> *I'm a sick man ... a mean man. There's nothing attractive about me. I think there's something wrong with my liver. But, actually, I don't understand a damn thing about my sickness; I'm not even too sure what it is that's ailing me. I'm not under treatment and never have been, although I have great respect for medicine and doctors. Moreover, I'm morbidly superstitious—enough, at least, to respect medicine. With my education I shouldn't be superstitious, but I am just the same. No, I'd say I refuse medical help simply out of contrariness. I don't expect you to understand that, but it's so. Of course, I can't explain whom I'm trying to fool this way. I'm fully aware that I can't spite the doctors by refusing their help. I know very well that I'm harming myself and no one else. But still, it's out of spite that I refuse to ask for the doctors' help. So my liver hurts? Good, let it hurt even more!*

As you can see, the intensity of the first line is lived up to in the rest of the paragraph; the entire opening paragraph acts as a hook and serves to propel us more strongly into the text.

Here's another good example, this one from modern literature, from 'Golden', the opening story of the collection *Nude in Tub*, by G.K. Wuori:

> *To die in winter in a far northern place is to become a storage problem. An uncomfortable building, only slightly heated, keeps the departed fresh for spring interment, although the affluent can opt for the dynamite and backhoe method of winter burial, not permitted in truly old cemeteries.*

After an opening paragraph like this—so exotic and detailed—who could possibly put the story down? 'Hook' is an apt term because it works like a fishhook: if you barely hook a fish, say, by the edge of his lip, there is a chance he'll get away. But if you hook him deeply, say, through his entire cheek, he is yours.

Most writers think hooks need to be intense, eye-catching. This is a misconception and often what results is overcompensation. On the contrary, the job of the hook is to set the tone for the book; if your opening line is intense, you set yourself up for a hard act to follow. What's impressive to the professional reader is not initial intensity but *maintained* intensity, which indicates endurance and patience. It shows a manuscript well thought out, instead of unfolding off the top of a writer's head. Ironically, I often find that manuscripts with more subdued openings end up being the best; the opening line may be less shocking, but I am also not set up then disappointed by what follows. These writers don't write an opening for the sake of an opening, but for the sake of the story that follows. There is a world of difference between the two.

The employment of a hook at the close of a paragraph, page, or chapter, where it can be at least as effective, is often neglected (a major oversight). The feat for a writer is to produce a piece of writing so strong that the reader, after putting the book down at a chapter break (where he normally does), will want to come back to it and reinvolve himself in its world, in essence, putting in the effort to start again. One of the most effective ways of doing this is with a strong closing hook that either, ideally, propels the reader directly into the next chapter, or at the very least resonates with him so that he will *have* to come back to see what happens.

Writers with some notion of this idea think a strong closing line is all that's needed. Another big misconception. Everything in writing is cumulative. Even if there's a strong last line or paragraph, if what's come before is bland, the reader will still put the book down. It is like a bad soap opera that is slow and bland but ends with a dramatic or shocking moment. Most often, this moment in and of itself is not enough; we will not tune in tomorrow because, while that moment may have been interesting, we don't care about all that's come before. The TV show *Batman*, on the other hand, was a totally different case: each episode was set up so that there was no way one could wait to see what happened next. But this wasn't just due to the inescapable situation Batman found himself in at the end; it was mainly due to what happened before, to the *cumulative* events that set him up for this peak situation.

Solutions

The misuse of hooks is fairly common—common enough to give it early placement in Part III of this book, but generally not damaging enough to warrant its placement with the preliminary problems. Hooks are among those things that, if neglected, won't hurt too much, but if handled well, could have helped.

The current popular misconception is that hooks are synonymous with marketing gimmicks (thus the often found discrepancies between hooks and the body of text). Bearing testimony to this are the hordes of query letters agents and editors receive from writers who actually quote their own first lines in the cover letter. Have hooks become synonymous with advertising?

- The most common problem is a hook that stands on its own, in the worst sense. In this case, the text that follows seems to be of a whole different work, and in retrospect the hook seems more of a one-liner, a gimmick to catch attention. The reason this is so is because the hook really is not part of the text.

The solution therefore is to bridge the gap, to make the hook and text integral to each other. This can be done by either starting again with the same hook and creating a new text that grows out of it, or working backwards, keeping the text you've written and writing a new hook. Incidentally, I'm not advocating bland hooks; the challenge is to have the provocative hook but at the same time not have the discrepancy.

This applies equally to hooks at the end of chapters. Many chapters culminate in what feel like tacked-on endings. You mustn't decide when you reach the last paragraph to end with a punch—rather, you must decide to end with a punch from the first sentence of the manuscript. That way, you can lead up to it, and when you reach it, it will not feel rushed or tacked-on. Writers today seem to think a dramatic ending is to be executed in one line or paragraph; the fact is that a good ending can be consummated over the course of many pages. This again goes back to the issue of stamina, endurance, and concentration, which must be built into the writer, as with any other artist.

- A variation on this problem is the hook at one with the text but disproportionate in terms of intensity or hyperbole—the 'over-excited' hook. This is a danger because it sets us up for more than we get. What if, for instance, in the previous example from *Notes from Underground*, after 'I'm a sick man ... a mean man' the rest of the paragraph were completely normal, monotone, reserved? If this is your problem, then the solution again is to work on bridging the gap; but this is more easily fixed—the gap need not be bridged in terms of content necessarily, but more by the hook being smoothed out or toned down.

- Another common problem is the use of dialogue as an opening hook. This is hard to pull off and almost never works, especially with beginning writers. The main problem is that exposition is needed to establish a story and so must eventually separate this dialogue from the rest of the text. Thus, on its own, this dialogue calls too much attention to itself, feels like a ploy. Opening with dialogue is also melodramatic (hooks are inherently dramatic and thus should be played against) and is often a cop-out for a real hook.

- Finally, there is the complete absence of any hook (opening or closing). If this is the case, practise creating them. Read other texts to see as many examples as you can. Take chances—start and end with a bang. If this is your problem, your overriding concern should be a reader's not setting your book down.

Examples

John killed three people and didn't stop to think twice about it. Raised with three brothers and two sisters, he grew up in a small town in South Dakota. His parents were Baptists. His upbringing was normal. He lived a decent, healthy life ….

Here you have the hook out of place with the rest of the text. The material that follows is even of a totally different subject matter! There is too much of a contrast and no transition, jarring the reader, who may feel angry, as if the first line was only a gimmick.

'You can take this job and shove it!' John yelled.

John was red in the face. He was huffing and puffing and pacing around his boss's office. His boss sat at his desk, not moving. John kicked over some chairs. John had been working there a very long time. This had been a long time coming.

Here we have the dialogue used as hook (clichéd dialogue at that, which usually comes hand in hand with these types of hooks). Note how the dialogue must be interrupted in order to fill the reader in, to set up the book, e.g. 'John had been working there a very long time.' This is always the case: a book *has* to be set up, so the writer who uses dialogue as a hook often falls into this trap. Note also the melodramatic dialogue, usually synonymous with dialogue as hook.

Mary was walking her dog. It was a large golden retriever. She liked to take him for walks through the park. It was a sunny day. Nothing much was happening.

Here we have an example of no hook at all. Who cares if Mary was walking her dog? We walk our dogs every day—we certainly don't want to read about someone else walking theirs. You can just imagine the voice this might be read in—droning, monotone, bored. It comes through in the prose.

End-of-Chapter Exercises

In an attempt to get you to apply the intensity of your hook to your manuscript as a whole, think of hooks in a completely new way: not just to be used as openings and closings of chapters but also as openings and closings of line breaks, of paragraphs, and ultimately even of sentences. Pretend the paragraph at hand, no matter where it falls in your book, is the opening of your novel: pretend the paragraph's closing is your book's finale. You'll see how this not only influences the paragraph's opening and closing, but everything between. When you work on hooks, the text between them will take on a more focused feel, propelled from an opening and leading to a closing. This should add an extra layer of intensity to your manuscript.

15

Subtlety

Many novelists think that, if only they can get published, break into print, then they will have made it, then all their worries will be over. This is far from the truth. Many successfully published writers must still keep day jobs in order to support themselves. It is unfortunate, because the press tends to publicize only those writers selling millions of copies, and thus the public is inevitably presented with a skewed picture of the publishing industry. Most books do not sell more than 10,000 copies. In 1996, only eleven hardcover titles in the USA—out of some 50,000 new books—sold over a million copies.

ALTHOUGH the focus of this book is what can be wrong in a manuscript, if we were to stop and ask what best signals the proficient writer, the answer would be subtlety. Subtlety is the mark of confidence and is thus by far the hardest thing for a writer to achieve. A writer who is confident need not prove anything, need not try to grab attention with spates of stylism or hyperbole or melodrama. A writer who is subtle is in no rush; he can pace himself, prolong tension, suspense, and even dialogue for hundreds of pages. He can hint, foreshadow ever so slightly, set things up hundreds of pages in advance. He will often leave things unsaid, may even employ a bit of confusion, and often allow you to come to your own conclusions.

Many commercial writers are less than subtle. Reading these writers is like eating a bar of chocolate: It may satisfy you temporarily, but in the long run it leaves little substance. You'll get a quick high but then come crashing down after you're through; you will most likely forget their work completely within a few weeks. The subtle writer, on the other hand, may not impress you at first—you may not even like his book until you've read it repeatedly; but, if handled well, the book will resonate with you for a long time to come.

You would think subtlety would come last in evaluating a manuscript, but actually it is far from last. When handled proficiently, it can indeed take hundreds of pages to evaluate, but in its mishandling, the unsubtle writer can often be detected immediately. The unsubtle writer will condescend to the reader, hit him over the head with obvious information, tell him things he already knows, and generally repeat things (sometimes to the word). The unsubtle writer should also see Chapter 11, 'Showing Versus Telling', as he will often employ telling—but unlike the writer who merely tells instead of shows, the unsubtle writer will often tell *in addition* to show! The unsubtle manuscript will have an 'inflated' feel—inflated with superfluous words, phrases, dialogue, and run-on scenes (the equivalent of run-on sentences), scenes that should have ended pages ago. These writers need a good director to say, 'Cut! End scene! *End* scene!'

Solutions

The main lesson the unsubtle writer must learn is that less is always more. These writers will often argue to their deathbeds that such and such information absolutely *needs* to be included; they will say, Think of the consequences if the reader doesn't know such and such. But they never stop to consider the other consequence, the consequence of the reader knowing too much. They don't realize that, when you underestimate a reader, you alienate him. If you had to choose, would you have a book full of information, or a book that will be read?

- Achieving subtlety is all about gaining confidence, not only in yourself but in the reader. You must raise the reader's standards in your mind's eye. Picture the reader as brilliant, perceptive, having a photographic memory, taking everything in the first time he reads it, able to grasp ideas before you even begin to say them, able to see where things are leading before you begin to lay them out. Usually how the writer views the reader is just a projection of how he views himself. The more confident he becomes about his own abilities, the more confident he will become about the reader's, so again the solution is to focus on building your own confidence as a writer.
- When it comes down to it, most subtlety problems can be solved by cutting. Of course, it is the art of where, how, and why to cut that this writer must master. It can take time to become proficient in detecting and cutting your own excess, and even the most proficient will not be able to catch it all. You will need an astute outside reader to point out what's overdone, what's extraneous.
- Look back over your manuscript and ask yourself if you spell anything out, if you are too blatant. (It is the equivalent of someone telling you an obvious joke and then slowly winking several times to hammer in the point.) If so, cut and replace with something more low-key.
- Look back over your foreshadowing (if any) and consider if, in the context of your book as a whole, it might be too overt. If so, there are three basic ways you can tone it down: (1) cut back the sheer space devoted to it; (2) make it more cryptic; and (3) move it further from the event it foreshadows.

- Look back over your text and see if you have a tendency to tell everything right away, to unfold your plot immediately. If so, discipline yourself to withhold information. Remember: most novels average between two hundred and fifty and three hundred and fifty pages. You have plenty of time. Take the pressure off and slow down the pacing (see Chapter 19, 'Pacing and Progression').
- Ask yourself if everything is too neat and tidy in your manuscript, spelled out perfectly; if so, there may be a lack of subtlety. You must allow yourself to embrace confusion, unresolve. Let some things linger, remain unsaid.
- Go back over your scenes. Are any of them run-ons? Can any of them be ended earlier? Can they begin later? What would happen if you ended a scene right in the middle, or began it in the middle? What would be lost? What gained? Usually, there is room for at least some cutting.
- Finally, when you think you are done, when you think you may have the most perfectly subtle manuscript, ask yourself this question: Will a reader want to read your book twice? Three or more times? If not, why not? If so, what will he gain from an additional reading? Most writers want to be reread. Therein lies the answer to how your book can become more subtle.

Examples

'Get the hell out of my house!' she screamed, throwing things at him. **She was angry with him and wanted him to leave.**

'I'm not going anywhere!' he yelled back. **He was intransigent, insistent on not leaving.**

'If you don't, I'll call the police!' she said. **She was threatening him and she meant it.**

'Go ahead and call them! See if I care!' he answered. **He was calling her bluff.**

> *The two of them were having a domestic argument. They were yelling and screaming at each other. She was threatening him and he was calling her bluff.*

Here's an example of unsubtlety in the form of telling *in addition* to showing. For instance, after her dialogue in line 1, we know she's angry at him and wants him to leave. The bold sentence that follows is unnecessary. The same holds true for the rest of the bold passages: we already know what they're telling us by virtue of what we've seen. Note how unsubtlety often comes hand in hand with telling, and how it also leads to repetition. Note how patronized you feel as a reader. Does this writer think we're in kindergarten? Does he think his points are that hard to grasp?

> *'Give me the cash!' Butch yelled.* **Butch was holding up a bank.** *'Aaaah!' screamed the teller.* **She was afraid.** *She was crying. Butch reached over and grabbed the money. He stuffed it into his pockets and then ran out the door.*
>
> *Butch was in the street and on the run.* **He was a bank robber. He was running from the police.** *He made it to his car and hit the gas.*
>
> *Butch was tearing off down the highway ....*

In addition to the superfluous passages (bold, as in the first example), here we have an example of a book opening with the plot. There is no lead-in, no let-down—we are hurled into it. It is as unsubtle as could be. You can also feel the frenzy behind it, the too-fast pace. (See also Chapter 19, 'Pacing and Progression'.) This writer needs to slow down; he writes now as if his book must be finished in one page.

> *John walked into the house and sat on the couch. Mary was already home, getting dinner ready.*
> *'How was your day, Mary?' John asked.*

'Fine, John. How was work?' Mary asked.

'Fine, Mary.'

'Oh, that's good, John.'

John got up and sat at the table with Mary. They ate corn and green beans and mashed potatoes. John told her how good it was and Mary said thank you.

'Mary, there's something I need to tell you,' John said.

Mary looked at him.

'I slept with your best friend today, Nancy.'

Mary scowled. 'John! How could you! I hate you!'

'I'm sorry, Mary,' John said. Mary got up and walked out the door, slamming it behind her.

John cleared the table and did the dishes. He went upstairs and made his bed and then he went to sleep. Before he did, he read for a while, then turned off the lamp.

The real scene here is what comes between the bold passages; all else is run-on, extraneous, unimportant. Having it there actually detracts from the scene, dilutes its power at both ends. In this example, we also find unsubtlety at work in other ways: note how the characters use each other's names in the dialogue (which they would never do in real life) and how John tells Mary that her best friend is Nancy, which he would also not do.

End-of-Chapter Exercises

Take a scene that you have determined to be excessive and rewrite it in an exceedingly minimalist, mysterious way, with no need to convey information. How would the scene unfold if the reader already knew everything you're telling him? You will be surprised at how much you can do with so little.

16

Tone

In 1969, *Steps*, a novel by Jerzy Kosinski, won the National Book Award. Six years later a freelance writer named Chuck Ross, to test the old theory that a novel by an unknown writer doesn't have a chance, typed the first twenty-one pages of *Steps* and sent them out to four publishers as the work of 'Erik Demos'. All four rejected the manuscript. Two years after that, he typed out the whole book and sent it, again credited to Erik Demos, to more publishers, including the original publisher of the Kosinski book, Random House. Again, all rejected it with unhelpful comments—Random House used a form letter. Altogether, fourteen publishers (and thirteen literary agents) failed to recognize a book that had already been published and had won an important prize.

From *Rotten Reviews*

THE distinction between sound, style, and tone is a subtle one. The way I define them, sound (as covered in Chapter 3) has to do mainly with the basic construction of the sentence—its flow, its rhythm—and is more of a technical issue; style (as covered in Chapter 5) also has to do with sentence construction, but has more to do with the intention behind the construction (e.g. florid, spare), and thus is as much an artistic issue as a grammatical one. Tone, on the other hand (as we define it here), has nothing whatsoever to do with construction or grammar—rather, it has solely to do with intention. Tone (e.g. witty, mocking, sarcastic, serious, intimate) is the voice behind the work, the driving intention behind the sound and style. Sound, style, and tone are related in that they all work jointly to affect the overall melody of a piece; but tone sits on the opposite end of the spectrum from sound, with style falling somewhere in between. Sound, or sentence construction, can be technically 'wrong', but tone can never be—it is always subjective, a matter of personal taste. A manuscript can have a perfectly skilled sound and style but an off-putting tone (such as may be imparted by a know-all narrator) that makes one want to put it down.

Even with this distinction, it may still be difficult to grasp exactly what tone is and how it differs from sound and style. It is sort of like the difference between tint, colour, contrast, and tone on your TV set: we're not quite sure what each does! All we know is that getting the right picture on the TV is a delicate combination of all of these factors.

Indeed, it is rare for a manuscript to be rejected based upon tone (thus its placement here, in Part III, as opposed to sound and style, which appeared in Part I).

Occasionally a manuscript has a blatant tone problem, and when that occurs it is virtually impossible to concentrate on anything else. For instance, who hasn't come across the overly personal narrator who is so intimate and confiding, who so takes for granted his relationship with you that you just have to put the book down? Or the know-all narrator, making cracks about everything, annoying you until you can't read any more? Or, conversely, the overly serious narrator, droning on in such a pallid manner that you feel as if you're listening to the speech of a funeral director?

Solutions

Tone is a choice, but sometimes we can be blind to the fact that we are *making* a choice and will need someone to point it out for us so that we can recognize it for ourselves.

- If you know you are taking a chance with your tone, or think you have a tone-related problem, or have been told this in the past, the first step is to show your manuscript to several astute readers and get their feedback. If they are unanimous in saying your manuscript has too much of a 'witty' feeling behind it, or is too 'sarcastic', then you've at least had the problem pinpointed for you. Identifying and recognizing it is the first half of the solution.
- Once the problem is identified, step back and ask yourself if your tone fits the manuscript. You must remember that a tone pervades a manuscript, fills its every pore. If you decide you don't like the tone you've used, what tone would fit best? Nostalgic, angry, sarcastic? Which is most in line with the overriding purpose of the text? With the narrator or protagonist?

Tone is an advanced technique, and it will take time to master it. If you're ever undecided, remember that the least intrusive tone is often the best course.

Examples

I was walking in the street and I tripped. You think it's funny? Well, I don't. I don't think it's funny at all. And I couldn't really care less what you think, anyway. I have a great story to tell here and you're just a stupid little listener. I don't know why I'm even wasting my time telling it to you—I have much better things to do. You probably won't even understand half of it, anyway. Figures. Birdbrain like you. Well, I'll give it a shot, but don't ask me to repeat anything. If you don't understand anything, look it up. You're definitely not going to understand my genius, but I'm not going to stop to explain it to you.

A blatant example. Can you feel the anger coming through, the brazenness, arrogance, condescension? There is nothing necessarily wrong with these things—they have their place and some people may even like them here (tone, as I've said, is subjective). But in this case it overwhelms the text, distracts us, and even goes so far as to influence the content, with diversions used to reinforce the tone. If this is not the intention of the piece, then this is a problem.

*Yeah, the situation was **just great. Just great.** My damn car wouldn't work and I was an hour late to work. **Fun, huh?** I had to listen to this dumb mechanic tell me all sorts of **lovely things** about how it needed to be fixed. I could have sat there **all day** listening to his **sweet words.** It was just **so fun. So so fun.***

Here we have a sarcastic tone, which is probably among the most common off-putting tones found these days (the bold areas highlight the sarcasm). In some cases this tone may work, but you can see how it quickly can become annoying. Again, the main point is to recognize and identify the tone that is being utilized. This writer may not even be aware of his sarcasm. Often the personality of the writer can leak through in the tone, and this must be fought. One must remember that a book is about its characters, not the writer.

It was a perfectly splendid affair with choice cuts of meat laid out ever so delicately and beautiful marigolds lining the terrace. We dined by candlelight and read Shakespeare out loud to each other. It was almost as exhilarating as listening to a Bach concerto. Winston brought us tea at just the right moment. We sipped and laughed and discussed issues such as the current election and the state of theatre today. What a marvellous night! We made plans for the following day to go bird-watching. Does life get any more exciting?

Can you identify the tone? Probably best defined as formal, precious, stuffy, serious, boring, self-important. Can you see how much it flavours the text? Sometimes you want the tone to suit the text and sometimes you deliberately want to play *against* the text, creating a feeling of contrast. For instance, how would a light tone affect a piece about a man on death row? A serious tone affect a piece of jovial festivity?

End-of-Chapter Exercises

- Take the first page of your manuscript and rewrite it specifically with tone in mind. Experiment with the following tones: happy, sad, angry, nostalgic, witty, sarcastic, mocking, important, trivial ... and any others that come to mind. Some may fit, some may not. The purpose of this exercise is to become aware for yourself of the influence tone can play so as to be more conscious of it.
- Look at your narrator or protagonist. What is he like? What would his tone be if he were telling the story aloud to you? Rewrite your first page with his tone in mind. Let him influence the text. Tone can be omniscient or character-driven, depending on the piece. Experiment with both.

17

Focus

Robert Penn Warren's first three novels were unanimously rejected by publishers.

WRITING is like steering a ship: one will inevitably—and constantly—fall off course on the way to one's destination. Did you ever sit down to write a letter and end up saying something totally different from what you'd set out to?

It is so easy when writing to fall in love with yourself, to let words, sentences, characters carry you away, to indulge yourself. 'Self-indulgent' is an epithet writers cringe at, but in actuality it is not such a horrible label: writers often have to allow a certain amount of indulgence in order to let their writing go where it 'wants' to, let their characters do what they 'want' to do—in other words, to let the work evolve out of itself. The alternative would be for the writer to impose his original plan on to the work no matter what, even if no longer suitable, and this would inevitably lead to a contrived text. More experienced writers can mask it, but an element of lifelessness, a lack of spontaneity will linger at its core. Still, when the indulgence is done, the writer must, eventually, focus.

It is the writer's job to distance himself from his work and then return to it with a merciless eye, an eye that ignores the beauty of the language, the brilliance of the characters' improvisation. This eye—the 'focus' eye—must mercilessly ask if the writing is staying on track, if it is doing what it set out to do. Sometimes, of course, tangents work. You might, for instance, have an epiphany midway and 'find' what a piece is all about and thus change direction—tangents can even help you stumble into the very source of what you want to say. But often they will need to be trimmed, or otherwise shaped, be it a word, sentence, or, in some cases, a whole chapter. Editing to stay on track, to maintain focus, is not a weakness, as most writers take it to be. It is an inevitability.

Focus is traditionally talked of in a broad sense, as in make sure your story stays focused. But few people know that focusing can be applied in both a broader and more narrow sense. Someone who is a master of focus in its broader sense might be able to open with a particular theme or image and then return to it three hundred pages later, coming full circle in the most subtle way imaginable. If done well, there will be a smooth, seamless transition, without it being telegraphed; it will catch the reader by surprise, make him say, 'Oh. That's right. The book opened with this.' When this happens, there is a miraculous, satisfied feeling. The reader suddenly feels as if he's read everything for a purpose, a greater meaning, that he's been led on an intentional journey. He'll suddenly realize he's been in expert hands all along, feel taken seriously for the time he invested. This full-circle effect of focusing can come in many forms, from the (more basic) thematically related prologue and epilogue to the (more advanced) reappearance of one well-placed, significant word.

In its most narrow sense, staying focused can also be applied to individual chapters, paragraphs, and even sentences. Everyone seems to understand that no book should be by accident: what you set out to achieve at the beginning should be resolved at the end, staying focused along the way. But people do seem to forget this when it comes to smaller segments like sentences, paragraphs, and chapters, where it is at least as important.

Each chapter must be thought of as its own complete unit, ready to excerpt should a magazine want it (indeed, this very chapter was excerpted prior to publication); the same holds true for paragraphs and sentences. Do you resolve in the end of the chapter what you establish in the beginning? Many writers don't; they just plug along, inserting chapter breaks wherever they feel their text can use one—sometimes completely arbitrarily. Writers often ask me: How long should my chapters be? Is five pages too short? Is forty too long? The fact that they're even asking this question indicates they're thinking of their chapters in the wrong way merely as dividers for a greater whole. Of course, a chapter needs to be part of a greater whole, but it also needs to be its own unit. The appropriate length is whatever length is necessary to accomplish whatever that individual chapter sets out to do.

The focus of individual paragraphs is equally important and is more often overlooked. Of course, there is always room for suspension of resolve, and not every paragraph can have a perfect beginning, middle, and end, but a manuscript full of paragraphs that begin on one point and end on another (never resolving the original point) eventually lends an unfocused feel. This especially holds true for non-fiction. Also, by resolving at the end of a paragraph what you set out to in the beginning, you transform the paragraph into a unit of its own and end up giving the reader a satisfied feeling as he progresses along the way.

An unfocused manuscript, then, usually manifests itself in prose, characters, or events that don't stay on track, that are introduced but never resolved (or, more rarely, resolved but never introduced). It lacks continuity, goes off on tangents, has an overall 'rambling' feel. Another symptom of the unfocused manuscript is beginnings and endings (of chapters, paragraphs, even sentences) that are not as strong as they could be, that feel slightly 'off'. How can we feel real culmination if we've ended up where we have through some tangent and not through intention, through progression?

Solutions

The most painful of all editing is when focusing a manuscript, as it often demands doing away with perfectly good writing. The edit's principle is this: no matter how good the writing, if it does not further the intention or progression of the work, it must be cut. (You can take solace in the fact that you may be able to use the unused material in some other work.)

- Look over the events (even minor) in your manuscript and check to see if they are resolved. Often writers introduce characters but never show us what happens to them, or they introduce a harrowing event that could influence the story, but we never hear about it again. This sounds like a basic mistake but is more common than you'd think—amazingly, even many of today's high-budget Hollywood films have inconsistencies and lack of resolve. These could have been easily fixed in advance by a good editor.
- Look for blatant digressions. You know where you've given yourself some sort of licence, be it for pontification or self-indulgence. Now home in. Are your digressions really furthering the plot or purpose? Can any be cut?

  Of course, not all tangents necessarily have to further a plot—some writers employ tangents simply for fun or philosophical asides. Indeed, some of the more profound ideas in literature have come from tangents that would be considered purposeless in the context of the book. Witness the following 'tangents' from Dostoevsky's *Notes from Underground*:

... an intelligent man cannot turn himself into anything, only a fool can make anything he wants out of himself. It's true that an intelligent man of the nineteenth century is bound to be a spineless creature, while the man of character, the man of action, is, in most cases, of limited intelligence.

I believe there have been moments when I'd have liked to have my face slapped. I say that in all seriousness—I'd have derived pleasure from this too. Naturally it would be the pleasure of despair. But then, it is in despair that we find the most acute pleasure, especially when we are aware of the hopelessness of the situation.

Or the following, from Melville's *Moby-Dick*:

Men may seem detestable as joint stock-companies and nations; knaves, fools, and murderers there may be; men may have mean and meagre faces; but man, in the ideal, is so noble and so sparkling, such a grand and glowing creature, that over any ignominious blemish in him all his fellows should run to throw their costliest robes.

Still, for the beginning writer, it is probably best for now to avoid tangents.

• Look at your opening. Is it distinct from the rest of the book? Don't worry, you're not alone. I call these 'nervous energy' openings, launched on a burst of the writer's nervous energy. It's not easy to write a book. Every time you're about to set down a word a million internal critics raise their voices and point out everything that's wrong. For most writers, it's harder to *start* a book than actually write it, especially since in the beginning they'll have to grapple with major issues like style, viewpoint, and narration. It can be paralysing. So, naturally, many writers launch their books on a fit of nervous energy. There is nothing wrong with this—anything that helps get the process rolling is fine. But after a point you'll settle into your style, viewpoint, and narration, and when you look back, you'll find some writing that is exaggerated. I have seen many manuscripts where the opening pages—sometimes even the first hundred pages—were completely off track, so we cut them and began later.

- Finally, beware the dangers of being *too* focused. If your manuscript progresses too neatly, is too rigid, too perfect, then perhaps you've overdone the focusing and need to allow some room for spontaneity, digression. Don't be afraid: you can always cut the diversions if you don't like them. Think of them as a tool for helping you get to the core of some other issue or possibility.

Examples

I wasn't going to take nothing from nobody. Damn right I wasn't, no siree. Let them try to mess with me, see what I'd do. They'd get it right between the eyes, and they'd deserve it, too.

I was walking down Lermont when I came into trouble. It was a cloudy day, not particularly warm, and I saw it coming a mile off....

Here's a nervous-energy opening. The discrepancy between the opening paragraph and the one that follows is obvious. Note also how the themes and subject matter of the two paragraphs are not connected.

I just love what's happening to the garden these days. The sunflowers are sprouting along the edges, the tomatoes are becoming ripe, the cucumbers just look perfect. I've been hoping for this for days. I can see some flowers coming in, too. I just hope the tree doesn't block out too much sun. **That tree's been growing there for years. It was planted by Doctor Smith, when he first moved into the neighbourhood. The neighbourhood was friendly back then, no noise pollution, no traffic.**

Here's an unfocused paragraph. It sets out with the goal of describing what's happening 'to the garden these days', and follows up nicely. But when we hit the bold area, it falls apart. (One could even argue that the sentence preceding the bold area doesn't belong there, but this could be left to artistic discretion.) Once the writer starts talking about the tree, the focus has switched and he should therefore start a new paragraph. He switches again when he starts talking about the neighbourhood. Note how one topic just segues into another, a perfect example of what lack of focus does. It is almost like stream of consciousness (which has its place, but must be done deliberately, not accidentally). Finally, you'll see the lack of focus extending even to the last sentence itself, where the writer begins by talking about how the neighbourhood used to be more 'friendly', but ends commenting on the 'noise pollution' and 'traffic', which isn't quite the same issue.

John loved to watch cats. He watched them in the morning, he watched them in the evening. John liked to look at all the different colours. He wasn't afraid of them at all. He wished he had one. He had always loved cats. **John's friend's name was Paul.** *John could sit there watching cats all day long. There was nothing he loved more to do.*

The bold sentence is a blatant example of an isolated instance of lack of focus occurring in the middle of the paragraph. This is a clear digression and would need to be cut.

End-of-Chapter Exercises

- To help focus your manuscript, forget the writing before you and instead summon your original intention when setting out to write your book. Go over each chapter and ask yourself what your goal was when you set out to write that chapter. Did you have any general ideas about where you wanted it to go? Did it go there? If not, where did you go off course? When you went off course, could it be the source of some other point? Does it belong here? Can you add anything to the chapter to help bolster your original intention?

- Apply the above exercise to individual sentences, paragraphs, and chapter sections ('chapter sections' are sections of a chapter as designated by line breaks, sometimes indicated by a few stars or other design element running across the page). Also apply it, on a bigger scale, to book or part sections, if you have any.

- Do all your sentences progress with focused intention to comprise a paragraph? Do all of your paragraphs progress nicely to make up a chapter? What about your chapters? View all these as pieces in a bigger puzzle and make sure they are focused as a whole.

18
Setting

A classic is something that everybody wants to have read and nobody wants to read.

Mark Twain

IT is amazing how often setting is neglected, employed only as necessary. This is such a mistake because, when brought to life, good settings can add a whole new dimension to a text, a richness nothing else can. They can affect relationships between characters and even serve as stimuli for new characters. At its best, setting itself becomes a character, interacting with the other characters.

Take a father and son, for example, having a casual conversation in their living room. Change that setting to a prison, the father and son having that same casual conversation on either side of a plastic divider. It's the same conversation, but it's not. There is suddenly a layer of subtext, of immediacy, of tragedy—and all without *telling* us a word. A writer's chief objective is always subtlety, to convey information without actually saying anything, and setting is one powerful way to do that.

Many writers sneak by with underdeveloped settings because setting, like pacing, is something established throughout the course of a book. This is why setting can take so much time for an agent or editor to evaluate and why this chapter is placed here, as the penultimate chapter of our book. Many writers, even published ones, get away with just a few lines of description for settings that are easily forgotten.

But there are some obvious setting mistakes that can cause a manuscript to be dismissed early. These include no settings whatsoever, settings described in a way that stops the flow of the narrative, settings that hardly change, settings that never come to life, settings with which the characters never interact, and settings that never affect the characters at all.

Solutions

- The most obvious error is when there is no attempt at setting whatsoever. The writers of these manuscripts frequently open with a burst of dialogue or action but never slow down to let the reader know where he is. Usually, writers who ignore setting initially eventually get around to it, but these don't bother. The effect is that the reader will never feel grounded or rooted. These writers haven't given any thought to how setting can affect a book. If this is your problem, the solution is to comprehend setting's significance (as laid out in this chapter) and begin to make the effort to incorporate it into every scene.

- Conversely, some writers spend too much time on their settings or devote too much time to insignificant settings, either of which can significantly slow the pace of the work. Establishing settings requires description, 'telling', and as with describing characters, it is a challenge to find ways to stop and describe them without slowing the pace. The solution is to keep in mind two things: (1) if you have a tendency to describe the setting all at once, try stretching it out over the course of several pages—readers can't take in all that information at once anyway, and a setting will become more real if it unfolds slowly; and (2) if the setting is insignificant in the context of the book, devote as little time to it as necessary. Settings are also like characters, in that the reader can only make mental room for so many, and you don't want to press him to memorize more than need be.

- Occasionally you come across a writer who is averse to changing settings; he finds one or two settings he's comfortable with and, like a mole in a hole, doesn't want to move. This is commonly found in playwrights-turned-novelists. Playwrights are disciplined to limit their stories to only a few settings and seem to have a hard time shaking that when they turn to other forms. This is a great mistake because limiting settings often ends up adversely affecting stories and characters, hindering them from branching out, from doing what they would if they had the space. It is like a painter used to painting on a three-inch-square canvas who is suddenly given a ten-foot-square canvas but still utilizes only three inches. These writers should realize they're using a different medium now, and if they don't use it to its limit, what they write isn't going to work. They must learn to take advantage of setting to its fullest, not to be afraid to have their characters travel from California to Peru to Russia, to get involved in high-speed chases spanning the country, if appropriate. It might also be helpful for these writers to watch more movies and fewer plays, as movies inevitably tend to take advantage of a broader range of scenery.

- Often writers make an attempt at settings, but they just aren't real; they're not completely absent, but they're not memorable either. Small touches can help bring these settings to life. Here are five possible solutions:

  1. Most settings are brought to life by the tiniest details: a stain on the carpet, a cobweb in the corner, a broken window pane.

Use these types of details—often flaws or irregularities—to help make settings memorable.

2. Draw on all five senses when bringing a setting to life. Smell alone can transform a setting: a room reeks of dead fish or rubbish or a corpse, or something pleasing, like incense or flowers. Likewise sound: a group of students anxiously await the *ringing* of a bell. Visually, lighting is important, as in real life: a dim room can define a scene, as can one that is too bright. Feeling, too, can come into play, if for instance the characters are trudging through mire and we *feel* their feet sinking into the ground, or our protagonist is being tortured and we feel him being sliced with a blade.

3. As in real life, climate can define a setting. This is often overlooked. A freezing room is as memorable as a hot one; a casual conversation, if set in a torrential downpour, will less likely be forgotten. Choose from myriad possibilities, from steam rooms to blizzards to more drastic, plot-altering phenomena like earthquakes and tornadoes.

4. Most importantly, have your characters *interact* with your settings. It can be something simple, like a mother involved with her kitchen chores as she's carrying on a dialogue, or something as dramatic as a man struggling for his life in a boat in the midst of a storm. One of the first lessons for the actor is to do an activity that will help him interact with the stage, to make his presence more natural. The same holds true for the characters in your writing. One way you can achieve this is to have something in the setting interfere with or annoy your characters, for example, a loudly ticking clock, or construction going on outside the window while the characters are trying to talk, or a gnat that won't stop buzzing in a character's ear. Or, you can have a setting help

your characters, e.g. a microwave bell ringing just in time to alert your character to an intruder's presence (*Pulp Fiction*), a postman dropping by just in time to prevent a murder, etc. The ultimate goal of your characters' interaction with the setting is to have your characters (and story) actually affected by the setting. Look at your plot: does setting have a hand in determining events? This can help settings become more real, become characters in their own right.

5. Good settings are distinguished from great settings in that the former will name details, but the latter will go one step further and use these details to make an impression. For instance, a setting can be well described by saying, 'It was a small, dark room, poorly lit and airless', but better described by adding, 'It was oppressive, like a tomb.' Remember that the best settings are there not for their own sake but as a means to making an atmospheric impression.

Examples

'Hey, Rick!'
'Hey, John!'
'Hey, Rick! Let's go to the movies!'
'Okay, John!'
'Hey, Rick! Look, it's snowing out!'
'Yes, John, I see! Let's run!'
'Hey, Rick! Here we are at the movies!'
'Yes, John! Here we go into the theatre!'
'Hey, Rick! That was a good movie!'
'Yes, John! I'm glad we're home now!'

Here we find no attempt at setting whatsoever. Note how the writer uses dialogue to convey what's happening in the setting;

this is as grave a mistake as using dialogue to tell a story. Note how, without an established setting, there is a floating, groundless feeling, no feeling the scene is really happening.

> *'Hey, John. What do you think of these latest financial reports?'* *Bill asked.*
>
> *They were in a restaurant. It was a loud restaurant. The ceilings were high and it was hard to hear. The silverware clinked and clanged. The waiters bustled by. The floors had dark carpets. There was a stain on one of them. Light came in through the windows. The tables had white-and-yellow tablecloths. The chairs were made of dark wood. The silverware had small designs on it. The water glasses were tall.*

Here's an example of a setting arduously described in such a way that it stops the flow of the narrative—in this case, all but bringing it to a halt. Writers who do this also tend to have bad timing: as a reader you want to hear what's happening next, but are stymied by the description. Note how much of the description is petty, insignificant. This writer thinks he's bringing it to life in the details (such as the vague stain he reports on the carpet), but he has chosen details we don't care about and that certainly are not memorable.

> *'I want a divorce!' yelled Mary.*
>
> *She walked from one side of the living room to the other.*
>
> *'Fine!' yelled John, standing up from his chair.*
>
> *'I'm tired of the whole situation!' yelled Mary, leaning against the wall.*
>
> *'Fine!' yelled John. He paced around the room.*
>
> *'Is that all you have to say to me?' Mary yelled. She sat down on the sofa.*
>
> *'Fine!' John yelled, walking out the door.*

This setting is barely there. We see John and Mary are in a living room—see a chair and a sofa and a door—but the setting never really comes to life. How is this different from any other living room, these from any other chair or sofa or door? This writer thinks he's having the characters interact with the setting by having them sit and stand and pace, but this is not interaction. This is a shell of a setting, one that's defined but will end up being as unmemorable as the dialogue.

End-of-Chapter Exercises

- Train yourself to look for detail in settings, everywhere you go. Practise right now, in the room you're in. Find ten unusual details—it doesn't matter how small—and write them down. If you think there is none (say you're in a bland room), then go even smaller, focusing on the cracks and scratches in the floor if you have to.

- Ask yourself: what's the impression I want to make with this setting? There are endless details you can focus on in just about any setting, but as a writer you should be conscious of the impression you are intending to make. For instance, let's say your character's room is filled with hundreds of empty bottles, half alcohol, half perfume. If you want to focus on his alcoholism, you might focus on the former, but if you want to focus on his penchant for perfume, you might focus on the latter—and if you want to focus on his trait of collecting things in general, you might focus on both. Now, with this in mind, go back over your room and write down ten details that support whatever impression you'd like to make.

- Look at your ten details. Can any of these actually influence a scene? How so? Take a scene and rewrite it ten times, each time using one of these details in such a way that it actually affects the scene. Maybe your letter opener becomes a murder weapon. Maybe your pen becomes the signing instrument of a long-awaited contract.

- Take a scene you've written and transplant it to another setting. How does the new setting affect the relationships between the characters? What subtext does it lend the action, the dialogue? What new characters might appear in your new setting? How can they influence the relationships, the action? This technique of transplanting settings can be especially useful to help spark you if you're ever 'stuck' or unhappy with a scene.

19

Pacing and Progression

Flawed and false storytelling is forced to substitute spectacle for substance, trickery for truth. Weak stories, desperate to hold audience attention, degenerate into multimillion-dollar razzle-dazzle demo reels. In Hollywood imagery becomes more and more extravagant, in Europe more and more decorative. The behaviour of actors becomes more and more histrionic, more and more lewd, more and more violent. Music and sound effects become increasingly tumultuous. The total effect transudes into the grotesque. A culture cannot evolve without honest, powerful storytelling. When society repeatedly experiences glossy, hollowed-out, pseudo-stories, it degenerates. We need true satires and tragedies, dramas and comedies that shine a clean light into the dingy corners of the human psyche and society. If not, as Yeats warned, '... the centre can not hold.'

Robert McKee, *Story*

WHEN you reach the point when you can't find anything wrong with a manuscript, when you've decided there are no egregious flaws and it's technically correct in every way, then you look to pacing and progression. The manuscript might he fine, but does it *read*? It might be on track, but is it slow? Boring? Is it leading to anything? Conversely, is it too fast? Are events whirling by? Are we racing towards culmination by the end of page 1?

A manuscript is such a tricky, delicate thing: even if everything else is perfect, it must not be too slow or too fast. It is like a soup: you may have included all the ingredients in all the right amounts, but a touch too much salt and the soup is ruined. Forget all the hours you spent chopping carrots and peeling potatoes—all the diner will remember is the salt. A manuscript must give us a satisfying sense of progression but not too easily. It must make us work—but not too hard. It must keep us turning pages—but not leave us feeling it is too much of a breeze.

Few writers comprehend the power of pacing and progression. Unlike other elements—such as hooks, characterization, setting, which can be dealt with in isolation—pacing and progression inevitably run throughout the course of the entire piece and are affected by every single last word. They are the central nervous system of the book. They are like a spider's web: tenuous, always ready to collapse, yet potentially strong, capturing and not letting go. One tear in one corner can bring the whole thing down, yet slight patchwork can strengthen the whole. Even the slightest reverberation in the most remote corner will be felt throughout: each strand is separate, but each strand affects the whole.

Pacing and progression are the most cumulative, most far-reaching elements of writing and thus demand the greatest long-term concentration. They require the ability to retain several hundred pages in your head at once, to be able to play with the idea that these fifty pages don't work, or the first two hundred pages are slower than the last, or pages 150–300 progress too quickly. This alone is a master feat, but it doesn't stop there: whenever you make an alteration, an adjustment, it again affects the whole and you will again have to start at page 1. But to make things worse, you only get one or two shots at it, because once you start playing with it, rereading your manuscript again and again, you will quickly lose objectivity and soon be in no position to do anything.

You will then have to put it down—for at least a few weeks—before you can come back to it. Clearly, pacing and progression are some of the hardest things to achieve in a manuscript. What makes this even more frustrating is that, at the end of the day, they are subjective: the reader of Conrad will react differently to pacing from the reader of Grisham.

Solutions

- Pacing and progression are among the hardest elements to self-edit. Generally the best solution is to ask your readers to read specifically for this. Ask where the manuscript lags, where it might be too fast, where progression might be lacking or forced. You'll be surprised by their reactions, because objective readers, especially in this regard, can often see things you can't. Note their comments—especially if there is a consensus—and reread problem areas with this in mind. Concrete steps (cutting, adding, usually plot- or character-oriented) will generally present themselves.
- Although it is difficult and may not yield the best results, it is worthwhile to at least attempt to self-edit for pacing and progression. This edit is something of a paradox. On the one hand, you will first need to get some distance from your work, take a few weeks (the more the better) away to get a fresh eye. On the other, you will need to get as close to your work as possible. While some criteria demand distance to evaluate, pacing and progression, after an initial distancing period, demand proximity. It is virtually impossible to evaluate pacing and progression by reading through your work piecemeal over the course of several weeks. On the contrary, it is preferable for you to read through the entire piece in one sitting, closely evaluating it as you proceed.

Now that we have the means for evaluating and locating problem areas, let's talk about some ways to fix them. There are no clear-cut answers, but there are some general principles you can follow:

- If you've determined that your pace is too slow, there are four major reasons why this may be the case:

  1. You've created a world that is more interesting to you than the reader (thus you feel no need to step up the pace, whereas the reader does). Be less solipsistic; assume for a minute that no one else cares about your world. Try instead to come up with a scenario that would interest anyone, including yourself.

  2. There is not enough at stake. If your first chapter is about four friends chatting in the living room, a reader may not be interested; but one friend holding the other three at gunpoint in the living room might be more riveting. We've touched here on an issue that really has more to do with narrative tension than pacing, but the two are closely linked. So if this tension is lacking, *raise the stakes.*

  3. Perhaps you have a good starting point and ending point but are taking too long to get from one to the other. Maybe some of the plot elements are interesting, but not interesting enough to be drawn out for two hundred pages—maybe instead we should get from A to B in fifty pages. This will increase the pace.

  4. You've used too much telling, too much description instead of scenes. If you cut back on telling and replace it with dramatization, where appropriate, you will greatly increase the pace.

- If you've determined your pace is too fast, ask yourself: What's the rush? Usually writers rush through their work because they are overeager to tell their story (often found in plot-driven novels). They rush because, while they may have a story, deep down they know they don't have enough material to fill in the gaps, to give the story a foundation, to make it come alive.

Another major cause of too-fast pacing is dialogue. Dialogue is the most powerful element that can affect pacing (see Chapter 6, 'Between the Lines'). Did you ever notice how quickly you turn pages when you get to dialogue? It's not just because of the spacing on the page. Dialogue, even in small doses, accelerates the pace, especially when coming after long narrative passages. Be conscious of its power and use it sparingly. (Of course, some books are filled with dialogue and read quite well—indeed, are classics—and the amount of dialogue palatable to one reader may be abhorrent to another. Thus, like everything else, this is subjective. But until you have mastered the craft of writing, I would recommend using less rather than more.) The vast majority of writers abuse dialogue, never stopping to consider they are disproportionately accelerating the pace. Books *can* read too quickly. One good way of monitoring your dialogue is looking to see how much you use in relation to the rest of the text. In other words, if you have one page of description and then twenty pages of dialogue, there may be a problem.

Progression is slightly different from pacing. Pacing is the measurement of how quickly you go from point A to point B. Progression asks: Is there a point B? Did you arrive anywhere? Readers need to feel a sense of progression—they need to feel like they're accomplishing something, like there's a point to all this. It's possible to have good pacing and poor progression. It's like flying a high-speed jet that circles the globe but lets you off where you started: the pace was great, but where did you go?

- If a feeling of progression is lacking, it may be due to lack of development in the plot, the characterization, to any of a number of things. Perhaps you didn't start the book with a clearly defined end in mind and thus are unsure to what event or culmination you're supposed to progress. This usually comes hand in hand with lack of focus (see Chapter 17, 'Focus'). If this is the case, the exercises at the end of Chapter 17 should be of help.

  Or it may be that you do have an end in mind but you're just getting there too slowly, which is a pacing issue. If this is your problem, and you like taking your time, one solution is to give the reader small points of progression along the way so he can feel satisfied and will keep reading even if you don't give him the whole story until the end.

- If your progression is too fast, too easy, remember: readers like to work. They don't want everything handed to them—they want tension to be drawn out. If this is your problem, you're probably underestimating your readers. Give them more credit; make it harder on them. As Emerson said, 'Treat people as if they're real—because *sometimes* they are.'

Examples

Mary was sitting in her apartment. She was looking at all the books on her wall. She got up and walked around for a little bit and then she decided to do some dusting. She dusted all the books and then she dusted the TV and then the pictures and then the windowsill. When Mary was done she decided to sweep the floors. When she finished with that, she sat back down and watched some TV for a while. When she was done, she turned it off and picked up the paper. She read the entire paper, from cover to cover. She sat there reading it for four hours. When she was done, she made dinner. When she finished with that, she got ready to go to bed, brushing her teeth, washing her hair....

Here's an example of pacing and progression both too slow. Who cares about Mary's domestic affairs? How do they differ from what we do every day? What's at stake here? We have been given no reason at all to care, to think this might be leading somewhere, and the result is a slow pace, certain to make any reader put the book down.

Russia bombed America. That was how it started.

There were fires everywhere, people screaming, floods, looting, you name it.

Then America fought back, bombing the Russians. Everyone was cheering in the streets.

Everyone was preparing for the next attack. People were getting ready.

A third war started. Soldiers were called up.

John was called up, too. He couldn't wait to go....

A too-fast pace. Any of these lines could constitute an entire chapter—an entire book!—and yet this writer's rushing through as if he has somewhere to go in a hurry. Note the quick, short paragraphs, a common symptom of the too-fast pace.

'I'm sorry, sir, I can't do it. I can't loan you five hundred thousand dollars.'

'But it's my money!' Dave yelled.

'No, sir, it's the bank's money now,' the bank officer reported.

'I'm going to sue you.'

'Well, go ahead, sir.'

'Call in the manager!'

'I'm the manager,' another man said. 'How can I help you?'

'I want my money!' Dave yelled.

'You can't have it!' the manager yelled back.

'This won't be the last you hear from me!'

This is an example of how dialogue can unnaturally accelerate the pace. You'll notice there is no break between Dave's asking for the manager and the manager answering. Dialogue can do that, it can bridge those gaps; but while it may work temporarily, too much will be left out.

End-of-Chapter Exercises

Here are some exercises that can help familiarize you with increasing and decreasing pace and instilling a sense of progression:

- Take one page (or minor event) from your manuscript and expand it into a fully-fledged story (about ten to fifteen pages) in its own right. This will force you to slow the pace, as you struggle to make what previously filled one page now fill many more. How might you expand your material and still keep up the pace, the intensity? What tricks must you use to increase the pace?
- Take an entire story (or major event) from your work and condense it to only one page. This will force you to increase the pace, as you struggle to make what previously filled many pages now fill only one. How might you condense it without making it read too fast? What tricks must you use to slow the pace consciously?
- If you suffer from lack of progression, here's an exercise that may help. As my editor so astutely reminded me, writers (be it novelists, screenwriters, journalists, even poets) are often unwilling to sketch out the action or events of their work in advance; instead they progress by instinct, relying on either vague plot ideas or the characters themselves to answer all their questions. This often works partially but not completely, and can result in alternate bouts of progression and stasis ('fast' and

'slow' sections), in a general lack of maintained progression, and in an ending lacking culmination. To prevent this, you might consider drafting even the vaguest synopsis in advance, in order to at least lay out a path (feeling free to alter your synopsis as you go along). At least you will be following some course, even if crude and transient, and this just may result in a manuscript with a fuller sense of progression—and thus satisfaction—for the reader.

Epilogue

A southern writer named John Kennedy Toole wrote a comic novel about life in New Orleans called *A Confederacy of Dunces*. It was so relentlessly rejected by publishers that he killed himself. That was in 1969. His mother refused to give up on the book. She sent it out and got it back, rejected, over and over again. At last she won the patronage of Walker Percy, who got it accepted by the Louisiana State University Press, and in 1980 it won the Pulitzer Prize for fiction.

From *Rotten Reviews*

G ETTING published is hard these days, even for great writers, even for writers who have been published before. With the conglomeration of major publishers and the fear of the 'mid-list' book, many fine books will never make it into print.

Do not be discouraged. If you stay with it long and hard enough, you will inevitably get better at your craft, learn more about the publishing business, maybe get published in a small literary magazine—eventually even find an agent. Maybe your first book won't sell; maybe your second or third won't either. But if you can stand the rejection, if you can stubbornly stay with it year after year after year, you *will* make it into print. I know many writers who wrote several books—some over the course of thirty years—before they finally got their first book deal.

You must ask yourself how devoted you are to getting published. Yes, a lot of the publishing process is out of your control.

You might, for instance, have just missed your big deal at a publishing house because a book similar to yours was bought the week before; or you might get the green light from every editor in the house and then get turned down at the last second because the editor-in-chief or publisher—or even a sales rep—personally didn't like your book. But a lot of the process—a lot more than you think—is in your control, and this is where devotion comes into play.

While the *craft* of writing has little to do with being social, I can assure you the *business* of writing does. Writers tend not to be social beings, but if you're serious about being published, this is probably the single most important thing for you to know: unequivocally, your biggest resource in getting published is other people. You may learn more about publishing from one party in one afternoon than from entire volumes. Some writers enter graduate programmes; they attend colonies, retreats, conferences, workshops, readings; they befriend dozens of other writers, establish a network that provides them feedback on their writing, information on the publishing process, and potential referrals and endorsements.

The answer, ultimately, to getting published is how much it means in your life. Does it take number-one priority? Some people give over their entire lives to writing. They give up their jobs; they write twelve hours a day; they apply for every grant, award, and fellowship out there; when they're not writing, they're reading literature, scrutinizing other writers' techniques, reading books on writing. Thomas Mann wouldn't even interrupt his writing to attend the funeral of his son, who had killed himself.

Genet was forced to write on toilet paper, as that was all he had during his many years in prison. When the guards found and destroyed his life's work, he began again, recreating what he'd done from memory. Dostoevsky spent many years in a prison camp in Siberia, where he wasn't allowed to read anything but the Bible and was given no writing materials—just hard labour. But he continued to write when he got out, despite the fact that Russian law prohibited a former prisoner to be published. When the tsar read Dostoevsky's *House of the Dead*—given to him by friends—he cried, lifted the ban, and allowed the work to be published. Conrad, a Polish refugee, taught himself English while working on a ship, despite the fact that he didn't speak a word of it until he was twenty years old. Through sheer devotion, he turned himself not only into a proficient writer but into one of the great masters of the English language. Faulkner laboured in factories and post offices while he wrote his works. He said the great thing about being published was that he was 'no longer at the mercy of every bastard who had five cents for a stamp'.

If these writers could overcome such obstacles, how can you give up after a few rejection slips? If you've made it this far, taken the time to read this book through, you've already exhibited a devotion surpassing that of many writers.

The ultimate message of this book, though, is not that you should strive for publication, but that you should become devoted to the craft of writing, for its own sake. Ask yourself what you would do if you knew you would never be published. Would you still write? If you are truly writing for the art of it, the answer will be yes. And then, every word is a victory.

Noah Lukeman is author of several books on the craft of writing, including *The Plot Thickens: 8 Ways to Bring Fiction to Life* and *The Art of Punctuation*. His critically acclaimed books have been selections of multiple book clubs, Book Sense 76 picks, *Publishers Weekly Daily* picks, and translated into Japanese, Portuguese, Korean, Turkish, Chinese, and Indonesian. He is also author of the original play, *The Tragedy of Macbeth, Part II: The Seed of Banquo*, recently published in the US, and his screenplay, *Brothers in Arms*, is in pre-production and set to film in Europe in 2010. He has contributed to *Poets & Writers, Writers Digest, The Writer, AWP Chronicle*, and *The Writers Market*, and has been anthologized in *The Practical Writer* (Viking).

Noah is also President of Lukeman Literary Management Ltd, a New York-based literary agency, which he founded in 1996. His clients include winners of the Pulitzer Prize, American Book Award, Pushcart Prize, and O. Henry Award, finalists for the National Book Award, Edgar Award, Pacific Rim Prize, multiple *New York Times* bestsellers, national journalists, major celebrities, and faculty of universities ranging from Harvard to Stanford. He has worked as a Manager in the New York office of Artists Management Group, Michael Ovitz's multi-talent management company, and for another New York literary agency. Prior to becoming an agent he worked on the editorial side of several major publishers, including William Morrow and Farrar, Straus, Giroux, and as editor of a literary magazine.

He has been a guest speaker on the subjects of writing and publishing at numerous forums, including the Wallace Stegner writing programme at Stanford University, The Juilliard School, and the Writers Digest Conference at BookExpo America. He earned his BA with High Honours in English and Creative Writing from Brandeis University, cum laude.

Noah lives in New York City. You may contact him at www.noahlukeman.com

Index